IndyRef to

Campaigning for Yes

Peter Lynch

Welsh Academic Press

Published in Wales by Welsh Academic Press, an imprint of

Ashley Drake Publishing Ltd
PO Box 733
Cardiff
CF14 7ZY

www.welsh-academic-press.wales

First Edition – 2017

ISBN
978-1-86057-131-2

British Library Cataloguing-in-Publication Data.
A CIP catalogue for this book is available from the British Library.

Typeset by Replika Press Pvt Ltd, India
Printed by Akcent Media, Czech Republic

Contents

For Hilary Warkentin and Brooklyn Warkentin

Foreword

See they politicians at Westminster or Holyrood or wherever they are? They're no even here, they're up in space. See whit I want to dae wi them? I want tae get them on the nummer 14 bus. It should be obligatory. And no jist for a couple o stoaps. The haill bliddy route, start tae finish. It might jist make them realise they're boarn. It might make them think twice aboot the guff they come oot wi. I doot it, but it might.

James Robertson, 'The Nummer 14 Bus'. 365 Stories[1]

*I*ndyRef to ScotRef is an account of the 2014 Scottish Independence Referendum from an activist's perspective because, unlike the 'great and the good' and the campaign leaders, my experience of the campaign

The first Yes Stirling campaign stall in Murray Place in Stirling on 23rd June 2012.

took place on the streets and on the doorsteps, visiting local communities and talking to as many people as possible.

The book concerns itself with the grassroots campaign in Edinburgh – which unlike Dundee, Inverness and Glasgow, was a very much a No city on 18th September 2014.

This book is therefore not a diary of the referendum or a memoir of someone at the centre of the campaign – I was very far from the centre so it's not an insider account or of the internal mechanics of a national campaign. Instead, it's an outsider account – because my experience of the campaign took place 'outside' in the streets and on the doorsteps. It was all 'out and about' like Peter Geoghegan's referendum study (Geoghegan, 2015).

This book is about the grassroots campaign in Edinburgh, but its contents will be familiar to people across Scotland. For me, the campaign was fascinating at the academic level as well as at the personal one. Yes campaigners loved this campaign was because we were able to campaign

Yes Scotland campaign staff in Buchanan Street, Glasgow on 23rd June 2012. (Image courtesy of Alison Thewliss)

Andrew Scott, Gordon Wilson and Shona Robison at a Yes Scotland campaign stall at the Broughty Ferry Gala, 1st July 2012. (Image courtesy of Andrew Scott)

The March for Scottish Independence, from the Meadows to Princes Street Gardens, Edinburgh on 22nd September 2012.

Yes Scotland stall at Stirling University, 5th November 2012.

for what we believed in – independence – rather than just a devolved parliament or Assembly like 1997 or 1979. Instead of limited powers, we were set to argue for them all. There were differences of opinion on the exact form of independence – in or out of NATO or the UK monarchy and range of different policy preferences – but this was a very united campaign, especially on the ground as the pluralism of Yes was a virtue on the doorsteps as campaigners could explain their different reasons and routes to Yes.

Whilst, the referendum campaign was issue-heavy and campaigners could be asked any question on any topic because independence was such a broad canvass, the referendum was really about people in terms of both the campaigners themselves and the voters we talked to. It's worth remembering, this was the biggest Scottish electorate in history, as it included 16 and 17 year olds, at the longest campaign with the largest turnout for decades: an exceptionally high turnout that surprised me. We had lots of time and opportunities to talk to voters and, in retrospect, the referendum was one, long public engagement exercise: which might have some longer lasting effects. It contained very traditional campaign events like public meetings, canvassing and leafleting, but also a huge amount of social media and political carnival too. It saw the establishment of new political organizations like Women for Independence, National Collective and Radical Independence, some of which continued to grow after the referendum itself was done and dusted. And, it created tens of thousands of new campaigners and galvanized some of the older campaigners to hit the streets. This came across very clearly when my dad came out canvassing at the tender age of 79, ready and willing to tell fellow pensioners they should vote Yes for the futures of their children and grandchildren rather than simply think about their own bank balance.

The young themselves were certainly involved in the referendum, something obvious when you teach students who may study politics but not engage with it practically. I remember giving my introductory British politics lecture to the new first years on Thursday 17th September 2013: one year

Yes Stirling University students with their Yes Declaration board, 11th February 2014

before the big day. The lecture theatre was packed with something like 250 students, despite the 9am start in fresher's week. As I looked up into the crowd, I could make out the little coloured Yes badges. Red ones,

Journalist Peter Geoghegan interviews organiser Will Storrar at the Bus Party event at Waterstones in Falkirk, 29th May 2014.

blue ones, purple ones, green ones and pink ones worn by about 80 students. Generation Yes had arrived on campus and was to stay there. They rejuvenated campus politics and the political parties with the SNP, SSP and Greens getting a real boost from some fantastic students. The university featured a large, enthusiastic and dynamic group of Yessers. They gave it everything at the referendum and a lot of them continued to be politically active in a variety of ways after the referendum too. They were part of a generation who took politics seriously, in spite of all the challenges the world threw at them: part of a growing trend in Scotland in 2014 (Higgins 2014).

Introduction

This might be a book about political campaigning but anyone who has ever worked with the public the way we did will find parallels with their own experiences. Anyone who does door-to-door sales, charity collections, meter-reading, personal care, community nursing or a host of other activities or occupations that involve knocking on people's doors will recognize something here. You might know your neighbours but when you go out onto the doors you are often entering *terra incognita* – people you don't know, in an area you've seldom been to, or at least

The May Day parade on the Royal Mile, Edinburgh, 4th May 2013.

not in years. Moreover, when you go doorstep campaigning, you realize everyone is actually out, most of the time, morning, noon and night, on weekdays and weekends. You've no idea where they are or what they're doing but you can pretty much guarantee that most of the voters aren't in when you call. It's as if they knew you were coming.

My Edinburgh was one from my childhood into my student years, but it didn't really exist beyond that in any meaningful sense. For about twenty years, for the most part Edinburgh meant my parent's house, Murrayfield stadium and the Scottish Parliament building: a very thin version of the capital city. When I returned to live here, my experience of Edinburgh thickened – not least through spending time searching for somewhere to live and then travelling round the city to haunts old and new. The referendum campaign sent my experience of Edinburgh into overdrive through campaigning in my local area in all its variety and also through involvement in campaigning in other parts of the city too like Craigmillar, Leith and Moredun. What I saw was a city very

The symbolism of the panda (there were more pandas in Scotland than Tory MPs) used to full effect during The March for Scottish Independence in Edinburgh, 22nd September 2012.

different from the one I'd grown up in – bigger, more international, more flats, more renting, more cars, more people, more pollution and congestion. The city was more expensive to live in – and I'm not sure how people manage it – leading to medium term trends like housing growth outside the city in West Lothian, Midlothian and East Lothian. Despite all the growth though, Edinburgh remained 'villagey' – meaning it still contained lots of little village areas like Corstorphine, Davidson's Mains and Stockbridge, that maintained a real sense of local identity.

People were key to what we were trying to do at the referendum. In essence, we just tried to talk to them, either at stalls in the street or on their doorsteps: very old school political campaigning based around conversations and shoe leather. Public engagement was our big thing, to try to reach people and discuss the issues with them and let them see that Yessers were ordinary people who lived in their community, not the ogres painted by some of the newspapers. This simple practice meant we spoke to a large number of people and I'd hate to try to estimate how

Thousands gathered for the second March for Scottish Independence, held on 21st September 2013.

many – did I speak to 2000 or more over the long campaign? I've no idea really. But, what stays with you are the people you meet, both specific people but also the generality of meeting so many and the impressions they gave you. Sometimes, you met tired, resigned people – already in their pyjamas with the door bolted at 6.30pm, wanting to shut out the world and its problems. Global economic crisis, price rises and wage restraints would do that to you. Sometimes, you met elderly people, some with memory problems, some sharp as a tack, some seemingly wasting away with loneliness, their families far away and out of touch. Often we would have been the only person they would talk to that day and perhaps longer. We met a lot of those people all across Edinburgh, mostly elderly women, suffering from isolation and a lack of community.

But, we also met sparky, imaginative people, young and old. People with attitude and some very clear thinking. Two of the most memorable conversations were with a recovering drug addict in Muirhouse and a

Yessers from Stirling University at the second March for Scottish Independence, 21st September 2013.

Liberal Democrat homeowner in Silverknowes. Despite his slurred speech, the addict was able to give a clear political analysis of the Conservative government's approach to the poor, the effect of austerity and what would happen with a No vote: he didn't need to be able to read the runes to know what was coming. His family, friends and community were at the sharp end of the Great Financial Crisis and this was set to continue without escaping the UK (which meant saying goodbye to a Conservative Government): more benefit cuts and hardship would be on the way for Muirhouse. In leafier Silverknowes, the Lib Dem voter didn't want independence and didn't want the constitutional status quo but said he'd never forgive himself if he voted No and we ended up with a Conservative government. Both of these voters were looking beyond the short-term event of a binary referendum on one day in September 2014 to think about what was likely to be heading down the road afterwards and they didn't like what they saw. Rational voters like these were common, though you did meet irrational ones too. An elderly lady at the bus stop in Corstorphine one morning declared she would vote No because it would stop the Edinburgh trams: a bizarre conflation of two events, not least as the trams were up and running 4 months before the referendum itself.

The second thing to say about the referendum was that it constituted a huge challenge not just because it was so long but because Yes were always losing in the opinion polls, except for some surprising poll results during the last few weeks of the campaign. These polls lifted the mood as we gained ground on No, but I still thought we'd struggle to do anything more than sneak across the winning line. The reversion effect – whereby voters shrink back from a big decision was more likely to mean we lost even if the opinion polls had Yes ahead. From the outset, I had the feeling we were pushing water uphill – a view conditioned by campaigning in Edinburgh – however as support for independence was as low as 23% in 2010 and 32% in 2011 (Curtice and Ormston 2012) getting to 45% overall meant we pushed a lot of water uphill but never enough to win. Being in a losing position most of the time actually wasn't as psychologically difficult as it might have been, compared to grinding tiredness in the final weeks. From the outset, with few exceptions, I had been expecting a No vote. Partly, this was due to the opinion polls – which had Yes behind and often far behind – partly it was due to living in the No-zone that was Edinburgh West, but also Edinburgh generally. Occasionally, a Yes

Yes Stirling public meeting at the city's Smith Art Gallery and Museum, 6ᵗʰ March 2014. Speakers included musician and journalist, Pat Kane, and the former BBC political reporter, Derek Bateman.

insider would tell me that we were ahead in internal polling or making up ground, but it was hard to chart locally. There was also occasional chatter in the media about the need for Yes to get above 40 per cent on 18ᵗʰ September – to manage an honourable defeat that would at least keep the issue of independence and of Scottish constitutional change in general on the political agenda. But, with the exception of a few local communities where we campaigned intensively, it always felt like a No, though it also felt like we were picking up support and gaining momentum, just not enough to win. Sometimes it surprised me that we kept in the fight as long as we did.

A third point I should make is that I was an unlikely political campaigner at the referendum and not someone who was a member of a political party or even vaguely interested in joining one. Academic politics and media commentary and analysis had become my thing and, although some people may have assumed I was a member of a party, I wasn't. I was a convinced Home ruler though. The referendum would constitute my third referendum campaign, having campaigned for a Scottish Assembly in 1979 and a Scottish Parliament in 1997. The 1979 experience was a dispiriting one, as it involved a teenager campaigning for a flawed institution in a campaign undone by the 40 per cent rule:

yes, I'm still bitter about it. The Labour Party of the time did not cover itself in glory in 1979 either. The 1997 experience was much happier and involved cross-party working, materials from Scotland Forward and some DIY posters too made with paint and cardboard in the back garden. It also involved some of the easiest campaigning I ever experienced – going to every door in a part of Stirling without a list of supporters to make sure

Flats in the Gorbals, Glasgow on the week of the referendum, September 2014. (Image courtesy of Cameron Pow)

people have voted. They all had and had voted Yes. Before moving to Edinburgh in 2012, I'd had a few discussions about the campaign with Yes Stirling in its early days and attended the Yes Scotland campaign tour when it visited the town (they seemed to be hunting for ideas rather than giving us direction), but expected that would be it for me during the referendum. When you're an academic and have done media work for years, coming out of the closet to support Yes was something I worried about. I wasn't alone. There were a lot of silent Yessers out there in companies, public organisations and even in sport, worried about what would happen to their careers if they came out for Yes.[2]

The fourth thing to say is that the weather was fantastic through the campaign. We love to complain about the weather in Scotland and rightly so. Edinburgh may be a very windy city across all four seasons – stalls and banners were regularly blown over and we carried a set of bricks with us to prevent all our literature blowing off into the Forth – but we only cancelled a few stalls due to the weather. Two or three cancellations out of more than 70 stalls give you the measure of the meteorological conditions during the campaign. In the last months, over the summer of 2014, campaigning involved hats, sunglasses and sunscreen and the weather only turned bad in the last few days leading up to the referendum. Good weather was vital for a community campaign of street work and engagement as there were so many houses to visit. Some of the Saturday morning stalls had some shelter but we were often exposed to the elements. Wind, rain, snow and the cold were going to be our enemies let alone what Better Together could throw at us. Sometimes, we could schedule street work in areas with flats – with warmth, light and shelter – but these were in limited supply in Edinburgh Western and the outdoors campaign required reasonable weather without which our engagement would have been sparse and ineffective.

1

Archiving The Referendum

Whilst campaigning at the independence referendum was something I did not think I would do, archiving it was planned as a key activity even before it was certain to happen. I'd helped establish the Scottish Political Archive at the University of Stirling in 2010 with our new archivist Sarah Bromage and we had an eye on future political

Folksinger Citizen Smart performs on the Royal Mile, Edinburgh, at the second March for Scottish Independence, 21st September 2013.

A billboard advertising the publication of the Scottish Government's Scotland's Future white paper, September 2013.

developments following on from the SNP's election victory in 2007. Another referendum was likely after 2007, though on greater devolution rather than independence I had thought. The archive itself collects and shares material about Scottish politics from politicians, parties and campaigners and we've built up quite a collection since we began. So, we had one eye on a future Scottish referendum but, in the meantime, we set about the task of collecting and organizing photographs from the *Scots Independent* newspaper, political pamphlets from the 1940s onwards as well as the personal materials of George Robertson, the former Secretary General of NATO. George had material from his university days at Dundee, from years of trade union and Labour activism and from his time as Defence Secretary and at NATO, as well as host of stories about NATO, Defence Ministers, Kosovo and the military generally. He was always generous with his time and enjoyed talking about his experiences with our Master's students in International Conflict and Cooperation at Stirling.

Nicola Sturgeon and Peter Murrell visit the Yes Information Hub in Stirling, 26th April 2014. (Image courtesy of Roy Cunningham)

The Aye Inspired exhibition at the National Collective's Yestival, held in Edinburgh, 12th July 2014.

As the archive became more established, we began to focus on referendums and campaigning, with a series of interviews with campaigners and key actors at the 1979 and 1997 devolution referendums, plus a series of talks and exhibitions about the two referendums in 2012. We had a lecture series from Linda Gunn, James Robertson, Kevin Dunion and Dennis Canavan, a musical song workshop from John Powles plus a campaign materials workshop for young people run by the SPA volunteers in Edinburgh. We also toured our exhibition of items, photos and information panels at the Museum of Edinburgh, the Smith Museum and Art Gallery in Stirling, Aberdeen Central Library and at Crichton campus of Glasgow University in Dumfries. Now, when I say items – the archivists eloquently like to refer to this kind of thing as 'ephemera' – what I mean is campaign badges, posters, leaflets, pens, t-shirts, banners and not forgetting Doug Maughan's bottle of Referendum

Rachel McCrum performing in a National Collective event at the Scottish Storytelling Centre during the Edinburgh Fringe, 8th August 2014.

whisky from 1997. The idea was to show the colour and content of the two referendum campaigns, though this was much easier for the 1997 campaign than 1979: in essence, more material had survived. We also had a soundbox to play excerpts from the interviews – and when I say a soundbox, what I mean is a huge, immovable box, with a small sound machine in it that you listened to through a telephone receiver. It did prove unstealable.

Whilst we collected the 1979 and 1997 referendums material, we also began to grow the archive with photos and leaflets from the 2011 Scottish election and added personal archives from Dennis Canavan and Jack McConnell too. Some of the material was archived into formal archive collections, whilst a lot was also scanned and put online through the SPA Flickr site.[3] Flickr is in essence an open-access photograph-sharing site. We began on it with the black and white photos of the *Scots Independent* newspaper, then added leaflets, posters, meetings and events at the 2014 referendum itself. The Flickr site also proved popular, as it

Ricky Ross singing Wages Day at 'The Stand in the Square' during the Edinburgh Festival, 7th August 2014.

Stanley Odd perform at A Night for Scotland in the Usher Hall, Edinburgh, 14th September 2014.

sailed through 1 million views in 2012, then 2 million views in 2014 and kept on attracting viewers into 2015 (it passed the 2.5 million barrier when this book was completed). What do people look at on the Flickr site? Well, basically anything and everything – sometimes it's photos or leaflets from the referendum, sometimes black and white photos of the SNP in the 1960s or 1970s. The size of the online collection also grew from hundreds, to several thousand to over five thousand in the period after the independence referendum as we uploaded the mountain of photos and leaflets we collected during the campaign and then added the items people sent us afterwards too.

So the plan for 2014 was to collect referendum campaign materials at every opportunity – it was not to campaign. However, I ended up doing a combination, which was easier than expected as there were so many events and campaign opportunities. The trick was to use your camera

Frightened Rabbit performing at the Usher Hall during A Night for Scotland, 14th September 2014.

phone and just click and go at every opportunity: there's a group of street campaigners, there's a stall, there's a billboard, there's a public meeting, etc. Some of the photos ended up a bit blurred and wobbly, but we collected a lot of clear ones too. The SPA team also comprised the kind of weirdoes who actually asked for leaflets from street campaigners rather than give them a wide berth: and our enthusiasm for taking leaflets did surprise them. We attended anything and everything, snapped away and collected stuff that went straight into large brown envelopes for cataloguing to the bemusement of some campaigners. This meant we attended the independence rallies in 2012 and 2013, events by National Collective like Yestival in Stirling and Edinburgh's Summerhall plus it's shows on the Edinburgh Fringe at the Scottish Storytelling Centre, the Common Weal launch festival at the Arches in Glasgow, David Greig's *All Back to Bowie's* show in the Manhattan yurt at the Edinburgh festival, the Bus Party 2014 tour when it visited Falkirk and Stirling, the Jim Murphy Irn Bru crate tour, Rory Bremner and Gordon Brown's event

Lady Alba at the National Collective's Yestival in Stirling, 2ⁿᵈ August 2014.

for Better Together and the *Night for Scotland* event at the Usher Hall in Edinburgh on 14ᵗʰ September. If you'd told me in 2010 that SPA activities would mean I'd spend an evening photographing Eddi Reader, Franz Ferdinand, Frightened Rabbit, Mogwai and Stanley Odd all supporting a Yes vote four days before an *independence* referendum I'd have fallen about laughing. None of that seemed remotely possible back in 2010. The fact that the campaign was so long certainly helped us to collect a mountain of material and, the fact I helped crowdfund a lot of Yes activities had the bonus of adding T-shirts, mugs and posters to the archive too: this is where some of the Women for Independence, Common Weal and National Collective material came from. We got hold of photos from the Yes and Better Together launches and tried to place people at events by both sides to get balanced material, including at the counts on the 18ᵗʰ September. A lot of people were generous with their time and resources and some of the material will find its way into a future exhibition. In short, archiving was my plan for the referendum, not campaigning. Though, as you will see in this book, a lot of the SPA material has found its way onto the pages and reflect my own campaigning efforts.

2

Transported From Australia

A fair chunk of January 2013 was spent on holiday in Australia, visiting old friends from university in Perth and Sydney. I left on 15th January and arrived in Perth on 17th January at 2 in the morning. In referendum terms this involved staying with a Labour-supporting No and a SNP-supporting Yes on opposite sides of Oz. The referendum was a keen topic of conversation with each of them, with lots of arguments in Perth: particularly over the exact wording of the referendum question which, I didn't think mattered all that much in the grand scheme of things. However, the plan in Australia was simply to take a holiday, catch up with my friends and enjoy revisiting some familiar places and heading to new ones: this time, the forests and southern coast of Western Australia (Northcliffe and Windy Harbour amongst others) plus the Blue Mountains above Sydney. I followed the campaign from there slightly but hadn't taken a laptop so was basically just looking at small BBC reports on their website before heading back to a cold Scotland via Dubai airport on 5th February. When I got back to the flat, there was a Better Together leaflet lying on the floor in the hall amongst the mail. It set me off. It was the exact moment when I became a Yes campaigner – an unusual moment of radicalization, which sounds childish when I think about it now. But, in any case, the real question was whether I could actually sit out the big one – this wasn't an election after all, but something far more profound. Could I really spend it in the media and academia rather than helping Yes? Before long, I had bought the t-shirt, the Yes mug and pens and was supplying friends and colleagues at University and began to get involved in my local Yes group in Edinburgh from then on. What I tried to do then was quite practical. In a political campaign, there's only so much you can achieve and have to be realistic about it. Other people are running the campaign, the strategy, the messaging, etc., and most campaigners are simply foot soldiers involved in the grassroots campaign. So, the aim became to help improve the local grassroots campaign, largely through canvassing in local communities and working on the doorsteps to grow support for Yes at the local level: you know, the really glamorous side of campaigning.

A Yes Scotland billboard advertisement at Carrick Knowe, Edinburgh.

3

Understanding Edinburgh Western

The name of the area I campaigned in is a good place to begin, as it's confusing. Before 2011, Edinburgh West was the name of both the Holyrood and Westminster constituencies. Indeed, the Westminster constituency was originally created in 1885. Its boundaries changed from 2005 onwards with the reduction in Scottish MPs at Westminster from 72 to 59. This reduction was a consequence of devolution enshrined in the Scotland Act 1998 – and an attempt to address the West Lothian question rather than resolve it. It meant that Edinburgh lost a parliamentary seat as Edinburgh Central disappeared from Westminster (but remained at Holyrood) and was effectively dismembered, as its component parts were

Alan Bissett speaking at a Yes Edinburgh West public meeting held in the Newliston Arms, Kirkliston on 25th September 2013.

allocated to the surrounding constituencies. The result locally was that Edinburgh West-Westminster expanded beyond its original core to the East to take in Balgreen, Saughtonhall, Roseburn, Murrayfield and Wester Coates, right into Haymarket and the New Town. It also expanded South into Saughton Mains and Stenhouse and across the rail line out West to add Ratho. At the 2015 UK general election, this seat had 71,749 registered voters. The Holyrood seat was smaller with 56,338 voters in 2011 and was contained within the Westminster constituency for the most part. It contained areas like Blackhall, Broomhall, Corstorphine, Craigmount, Cramond, Davidson's Mains, Drumbrae, Drylaw, East Craigs, Forrester Park, Muirhouse, Silverknowes and South Gyle. But, the seat also contained towns outside Edinburgh – like Dalmeny, Kirkliston, Ratho Station (not Ratho – a confusion locals will not stand for) and South Queensferry. And, out of town was not to be sniffed at – with 3000 residents and growing in Kirkliston as well as around 9000 in South Queensferry, both areas of historic SNP support in the constituency. To make things more confusing, my local group was called Yes Edinburgh West but campaigned in Western.

When my family moved down to Edinburgh from Peterhead in December 1969, Edinburgh West was a solid Conservative constituency.

A Yes Edinburgh Super Saturday event at Tynecastle High, 1ˢᵗ March 2014.

And, we moved to Corstorphine Hill, which was doubly Conservative it seemed. The adjacent streets were populated by fairly ordinary people – which you can translate as meaning they sent their children to state schools. Down the hill, the people sent their children to private schools so that even a small area like Corstorphine Hill had a fully functioning and recognizable class system you could understand in football versus rugby terms. It still did in 2014. When we arrived in Edinburgh, the sitting MP was Anthony Stodart, who served from 1959 to October 1974 when Lord James Douglas Hamilton took over until defeated in 1997. He had been a junior Minister in the Scottish Office for a time and was subsequently a regional list member of the Scottish Parliament from 1999 to 2007. Ironically, though the Conservatives have slipped away electorally in the area, the party is well-established locally, with a long-standing office in Davidson's Mains: the only party to enjoy such status in the constituency.

The only successful Labour incursion in Edinburgh West came in 1929-31 – when George Mathers briefly held the seat before being ejected and becoming MP for West Lothian from 1935 to 1951. The challenge to Conservative electoral hegemony in Edinburgh West did not come from Labour though, but came from the Liberals and Liberal Democrats from the 1970s onwards: often in the shape of Donald Gorrie. Gorrie stood at various elections from the 1970 general election on (he achieved third place on 8% in 1970), became a local councillor in Carrick Knowe and his constancy helped the party to establish a base in the area that continues to this day, winning council seats and at Westminster and Holyrood. Despite the party's post-coalition calamities, Liberal Democrat representation in Edinburgh Western did not disappear. This constituency retained the only three remaining Liberal Democrat councillors in Edinburgh in 2012: a reflection of a strong base built up over decades using Focus leaflets and local campaigners from the bottom up through pavement politics.

Edinburgh West started to go Liberal in 1983, following on from the split in the Labour Party by the Gang of Four in 1981,[4] the creation of the SDP and the agreement to have Alliance candidates: combined Liberal and SDP candidates across Britain. This development propelled the Edinburgh West Liberal Derek King to an agonizing second place in 1983, just 498 votes behind the Conservatives. The Liberal Democrats stayed a close second until 1997, when Gorrie finally broke through as the Tory vote collapsed and the party experienced a Westminster wipeout in Scotland. Donald Gorrie triumphed with over 20,000 votes as the Tories declined to 28%. From then on, the Conservative vote began to slip away to a distant second and third at Westminster contests and Liberal Democrat hegemony was established at Westminster, Holyrood and local council elections until after the 2010 coalition was formed. Tory voters also defected to the Liberal Democrats at the 2015 general election to fend off the SNP – not that it worked.

Come the independence referendum, the political landscape in Edinburgh Western was a fragmented one – and not at all favourable to Yes. The Westminster election of 2010 saw the Liberal Democrats retain the seat with 35.9%, but with Labour in a good second place to mount a challenge in the constituency with 27.7%: part of the reason the seat started out as a Labour target at the 2015 Westminster election, as the larger boundaries were seen to help Labour's prospects. However,

A Yes car and driver at the Tynecastle Super Saturday, 1ˢᵗ March 2014.

the decision of the Liberal Democrats to join the coalition with the Conservatives in 2010 came with substantial political costs in the area and across Scotland. The Liberal Democrats had held the Holyrood seat comfortably since 1999 with no real challenge. Labour support in the seat was not substantial and the SNP only really achieved any level of popularity in 2007, when it came second with 22.4%. However, 2011 was completely different, as the SNP won the seat for the first time ever with 35.8% as both it and Labour put on votes from the fall in support for the Liberal Democrats and the Conservatives. The SNP gain was part of a national landslide, achieved through minimal local campaigning on the ground: attributed to extensive leafleting by a tiny team of around 6 activists plus the candidate. Before 2007, Edinburgh had been the electoral graveyard of the SNP: it changed with the new STV electoral system for council elections which delivered councillors in considerable numbers for the first time; the rise in SNP popularity generally; and the Liberal Democrat's demise after 2010. The Liberal Democrats did extremely badly in 2011. The only 2 constituency seats it held were in Orkney and Shetland, whilst it polled so badly in Edinburgh and the Lothians that it didn't win any seats on the regional list.

However, when you reorganize electoral performance into the world of Yes versus No, you can grasp the scale of the political dynamics on the ground. First, the SNP was the only Yes party on the ground, with 35.8% of the votes from 2011 (11,965 votes) on a turnout of 59.3%: and not all of those SNP supporters were Yes, some were tactical supporters on issues of policy and government competence (Carman, Johns and Mitchell 2014). The remainder of the vote was divided between the three No parties – 21,487 votes in all. The Westminster outlook from 2010 was even worse – with only 13.2% support for the SNP and around 40,000 voters having supported the No parties. There had been occasional electoral forays into the constituency by the Greens in 2005 and 1992 and the SSP in 2003 and 2001 but neither made any discernible electoral progress and there was no organizational base for either party on the ground come the 2014 independence referendum to assist the Yes campaign. The SNP meantime, could muster one MSP and 3 local councillors and had around 200 members. Not a great basis for a Yes vote in a hostile political environment.

Second, and very simply, Edinburgh Western lacked Labour voters and also working class voters – though these are not necessarily the

Grahame Case of Yes Edinburgh West and his crowdfunded Edinburgh Yes trailer, February 2014.

same thing. One pretty good rule of thumb for a Yes campaigner was that if you had Labour voters, you had a pretty good chance of getting Yes voters. Sure enough, there were 7,164 Labour voters at the Holyrood election of 2011 and 12,811 Labour voters at Westminster in 2010, but the Conservatives and Liberal Democrats also had considerable vote shares and the Labour vote in Edinburgh Western was dwarfed by the size of the Labour vote in other parts of Edinburgh, let alone in Glasgow or Lanarkshire. There was only one council estate in Edinburgh Western – Muirhouse – though parts of Drylaw and Drumbrae also retained some council housing. Parts of Muirhouse experienced serious social problems and the area was also characterized by low political engagement and voter turnout: meaning Yessers might not be registered and even if they were, they weren't used to voting.

Third, demographically, and linked to the previous point, Edinburgh Western was challenging territory for Yes. Despite more fluid social classes in Scotland over recent decades, there was a clear social class profile to

Yes and No. Data for both the Edinburgh Western and Edinburgh West constituencies give some idea of the demographic patterns involved. Owner occupation was 72.6%, compared to a Scottish average of 61.6%, whilst the socially rented sector (local authority and housing associations) was 14%, compared to a Scottish average of 24.3%. The level of educational qualifications was 10% above the Scottish average at the highest level of measurement (level 4, meaning technical apprenticeships and National 4 grades upwards), employment levels were higher than the Scottish average and was strong in areas like finance and insurance (13.5% compared to 4.5% across Scotland), health and social work, public administration and defence and professional and scientific activities. In terms of occupations, Edinburgh West comprised 10.7% managers, directors and senior officials; 22.7% professional occupations (the Scottish average was 16.8%) and 14.5% associate professional and technical occupations. In socio-economic classification terms, the higher managerial and professional groups had higher % components in Edinburgh West than the Scottish average – which was reversed as you went down the socio-economic scale.[5] In terms of housing, not only was there a large element of owner occupation but, 28.61% of Edinburgh Western's housing was to be found in council tax bands F-H (compared to the Scottish average of 20.2%) and the mean house price was £233,050 in 2013, compared to a Scottish average of £162,266.[6] However, the local average is just an average. This is also a constituency of £500,000 homes and more, as well as of long driveways with security entrances too – check out Barnton and Cramond on the ESPC property website (Edinburgh Solicitor's Property Centre) and you get the picture. Not that there wasn't Yes support amongst the affluent areas, there was. It just wasn't of the same magnitude as support for No.

4

What Makes a Campaigner?

I wasn't the only person involved in Yes in my area who had not planned on becoming a campaigner. The local group had a core of SNP members, who had good local knowledge about the area but, for the most part, it was non-party volunteers who were active and this was the pattern across the campaign. In time, Greens and Socialists became involved, with occasional support from members of Labour for Independence too. But the volunteers were key. Some attempted to reinvent the wheel as campaigners, others brought skills, networks and determination to the campaign and coped with its DIY nature. In such a long campaign, there was time to get things wrong or at least, not quite

A National Collective photo exhibition at Yestival, Summerhall, Edinburgh, 12th July 2014.

right, but then to change them and adjust strategies and activities. It was one long learning curve. We had very few professional politicians in the area and the volunteers effectively became the 'unprofessional' politicians doing the campaigning, which worked well given how unpopular the political classes were.

The activists came in waves. And, in the last couple of weeks of the referendum, there were so many, we struggled to cope with the numbers. Initially, it was a small group involved in starting-up and getting Yes Edinburgh West moving into regular activities in the spring of 2013 – though the group was already running before then. Stalls began, some in our area, some in Dalry, Haymarket and Gorgie as our activism attracted people from surrounding areas. The group even managed a couple of stalls at Murrayfield to coincide with rugby matches. We also began leafleting and with it, the constant problem of getting material from Yes

The March for Scottish Independence, Edinburgh, on 22nd September 2012.

Yes supporters marching from the Meadows to Princes Street Gardens, Edinburgh on 22nd September 2012.

Scotland. Edinburgh West was one of the first active Yes groups, along with Stirling and Linlithgow and we were ambitious. If a new leaflet were available, we'd want to order 40,000, in order to cover the whole constituency. This industrial-style approach to campaigning came as a bit of a shock to Yes, who'd imagined us using a couple of hundred leaflets through soft campaigning at a stall on a Saturday morning. Instead, we were looking to ship tens of thousands and get leafleting in all areas of the constituency – even in leafy Cammo and Cramond and, even in areas out of the constituency. Our leafleting mastermind – Fergus Henderson – became adept at extending our coverage, remapping leaflet runs and swapping materials with surrounding Yes groups. If someone wanted to leaflet, Fergus would give them an area. If someone wanted some leaflets or newspapers, he'd hand them over, with guidance on street runs. Initially, small numbers of us were leafleting large areas

Nicola Sturgeon visits Yes Stirling campaigners on 26th April 2014. (Image courtesy of Roy Cunningham)

as well as taking part in group-leafleting sessions – don't ask me how many I delivered. Overall, the group delivered over 500,000 pieces of campaign literature during the referendum. Into 2014, there were so many people volunteering to leaflet that the individual burdens shrank and, in my case, disappeared.

When it came to volunteering, the most active people were the retired, though not exclusively. They were certainly a dedicated group and one with more time on their hands than most of us with work and family commitments. It meant that some campaigners were effectively full-time and some full-time across the whole campaign. Others amongst us were part-time though often it didn't feel like it. We also benefited from a range of life and work experiences on the campaign trail: meaning a retired doctor, accountants, social workers, school teachers, architects, business people, etc. It meant we had a lot of experience and knowledge for the doorstep campaign, which was necessary as almost anything could come up in conversation. We had some fairly simple Yes messages

Yes activists at a Duddingston, Craigmillar and Portobello Super Saturday, 7th June 2014.

The National Collective stall at a Yes Edinburgh Central Super Saturday, 6th September 2014.

and points to get across – initially based around the democracy, fairness, prosperity themes that were at the core of the Yes message from 2013 onwards – but any issue could come up, compared to a normal election. However, to some extent, whilst there was a facts and figures type of debate on the doorsteps with voters, there was also a broad values debate going on about what kind of country we wanted to live in and a fair number of voters connected to themes about social justice and a fairer society: broad themes in Scottish politics associated with every party except the Conservatives. This type of discussion went well four years into the austerity politics and economics of the Conservative-Liberal Democrat coalition government and was attractive to Labour supporters in particular, but also amongst Liberal Democrat voters who weren't fans of the coalition. This included the former local MP John Barrett, who supported a Yes vote.

What volunteers were prepared to do varied. Some were purely leafleters, who weren't comfortable doing doorstep canvassing or

Momentum for Yes was growing in Glasgow and activists were out in force on 6th September 2014. (Image courtesy of Ian and Helen Graham)

talking politics with voters at the stalls. Others were natural talkers and some thankfully, were good listeners too. We even had two different campaigners – Bill and Pauline – who operated as solo canvassers. You just gave them the canvass sheets and materials and off they went. The point of canvassing was not to turn up uninvited on someone's doorstep to give them a stern lecture on the benefits of a Yes vote. Rather it was to engage them in a discussion, get some points across and answer questions. We mixed up our canvassers regularly so everyone could get experience and see how individuals sought to make the Yes pitch on the doorsteps. We were always armed with material, including a good question and answer booklet borrowed from Yes Penicuik as we sought to plug the information gap to cover as many topics as possible. Before the Scottish Government's white paper on independence was published in November 2013, there was a fair bit of inexactitude about what the Yes political offer was in detail. Though, for a lot of people, this didn't matter, at least not at this stage of the referendum campaign. However, voters did want information so when one of our leading local campaigners Ian Grant got hold of a couple of thousand copies of the Yes Penicuik brochure, it really helped the doorstep work as a lot of people wanted some basic facts about what independence was all about.

What our local campaign group tried to do was broad. We had a huge amount of doorstep canvassing that revisited the undecideds and also targeted four areas again and again in Edinburgh West to increase voter registration, maximize support and find more undecideds. We also did phone canvassing in areas we were unlikely to reach personally, which involved some miserable times for those involved as they could see the size of the No vote. Leafleting grew to an industrial scale during the campaign period. Stalls were held weekly and sometimes several times per week. The stalls were there to give us a presence around the different communities of Edinburgh West (there was no one central location in the area), distribute literature, engage with passing voters and develop support: meaning collect signatures for the Yes declaration. The declaration was effectively a support and mobilization device – it gave us local contacts and emails to promote Yes messages and campaigning efforts and grow our network of activists. We also held a range of public meetings on independence across different parts of the constituency, featuring Alan Bissett, Liz Lochhead, Andy Myles, Ivan McKee plus elected politicians from the Greens and SNP. Some of these engaged

Yes Edinburgh West activists, including my dad (far right), canvassing undecided voters with Yes Scotland Chief Executive, Blair Jenkins, August 2014.

undecided voters, others were more successful in galvanizing our base of Yes voters and campaigners, though sometimes felt like an echo chamber. We also had visit from Nicola Sturgeon to host a question and answer session at Craigmount High School, plus a visit to Muirhouse by Jim Sillars in the Margo Mobile to mobilise supporters. We were also active on social media, using it as a public communications device to promote the case for Yes as well as to build a local network and promote campaign activities. We raised money on a number of occasions to fund the campaign, most notably to try to fund a campaign office for the last months of the campaign, though Edinburgh office rents and opportunities meant we failed. Instead, we ended up with a campaign bus for the last weeks of the campaign, loaded with campaigners and materials.

Of course, whilst we did the types of things a local campaign does – meaning organized campaigning – others took a very individual approach. Two university colleagues formed their own one-person campaigns to convince people to vote Yes. Bill Paterson gave himself the one hundred day challenge of having a different referendum conversation with someone new every day leading up to the vote. Kevin Adamson used the Facebook messaging function to launch discussions with FB friends but also, as a smoker, would discuss the referendum with the community of puffers created by the smoking ban in public places. As time went on, such conversations became more natural as everyone was talking about the referendum in the last few months of the campaign as politics moved from the private to the public sphere. Don't think this is normal. I can't remember this happening in any other electoral situation.

Yes Scotland briefing session for Yes Edinburgh activists in 2012.

5

What's Behind the Door?

Doorstep canvassing was one of the main activities we pursued at the referendum. We started this early – meaning in July 2013 – and continued in all the way through until the last week of the campaign, even after the Yesmo database was closed to organize the get out the vote operation, which meant we were running around mobilizing some voters on referendum day with handwritten lists. The early start was vital – we had no voter data at all to go on and tens of thousands of voters to talk to. We were armed with copies of the electoral register which would tell us who lived in the property, but this was often an uncertain and inaccurate activity. Put simply, lots of people weren't on the register either through dropping out of voting altogether – the 'missing million' – or through moving home. The combined effect of the housing rental costs of Edinburgh plus the fluidity of the rented sector meant there was a constant churn of residents. And, the effect of council house sales and extensive private renting had meant that we found renters all over Edinburgh in flats and houses out in the suburbs and beyond.

Anyone who does any kind of doorstep work will tell you stories of what they experience from the public. Every time you knock the door, you're not sure what is on the other side. It might be a dog – even a big dog. It could be a nice, soft lump of a dog or one that threw itself at the letter box the minute you got to the door. It might be someone who has just woken up grumpy as they're on nightshift and you've woken them. It might be a happy person, a sad person, a lonely person and even, an angry person. It might be a human in a state of undress or completely naked. By the end of the campaign, I was no longer surprised by the fact that many people would answer their front door naked or in their underwear – 'I'm just out of the shower' they'd say. Usually, you would have a name on the electoral register to provide some clue of whether you're knocking on the door of a couple, single person, large family or someone from the Asian or Polish community. Sometimes you knocked on doors with no information of the residents, specifically to try to get them on the register and here, we really were flying blind. We visited the blocks of flats in Muirhouse relentlessly for voter registration purposes, which meant we probably leafleted and canvassed the Syrian doctor who had amassed a host of explosive substances in Fidra Court in 2014 on several occasions: not that we knew that until after the referendum.[7]

But, the point about being constantly on the doors is the surprises you get. Firstly, very few people were rude. I can only remember one person in East Craigs who looked down their nose at us. Lots of people were interested to some degree though many were too busy for more than cursory chat. We met lots of No's, but they were seldom hostile. A lot of people were uncomfortable about talking politics on the doorstep, with some older voters stating it was a private matter and refusing to discuss it, but this became less prominent later in the campaign. Secondly, as time went on, people became more engaged in the issues around the referendum. Early on, meaning before the Edinburgh Agreement of October

The City Garden look at Salvesen Crescent, Edinburgh.

2013, some voters were skeptical about the referendum happening at all or knew little about it. So, to some extent, we were seeking to engage them in discussion about the referendum, not necessarily the case for Yes at the referendum. Gradually, through doorstep work, stalls and the extent of the campaign in the media, people began to engage with the issues at hand. There was no escape really.

Our task on the doors was superficially simple – we were asking two short questions. First, where do you place yourself on a scale of 1-10 if 1 is completely opposed to independence and 10 is completely in favour. This enabled us to figure out our supporters and opponents, but also a range of voters who were uncertain about the issue: perhaps the folk who wanted more devolution but might be interested in the independence offer – voters who could be tempted to No by more devolution offered by the Conservatives, Labour and Liberal Democrats, encapsulated in the Vow during the last weeks of campaigning. Second, we asked them whether they would be Yes, No or undecided at the referendum. Again, this gave a sense of the fors and againsts but also, the vital undecideds. In an area like Edinburgh Western we didn't run short of voters who were 1 and a No. But we also identified the *Spinal Tap Yessers* – those who told us they were an 11 on the 1-10 scale. Some voters enjoyed playing games with us, asking us to guess whether they were Yes or No and, it was usually impossible to tell: though it turned out it was usually Yes voters doing this. We also found a lot of undecideds who we revisited later in the campaign and targeted with special booklets and a mailshot. However, that was as sophisticated as it got. The other side – Better Together – asked more questions when canvassing including voter preferences, so could target their appeals to party supporters. Yes Scotland did provide some target demographic canvassing late on in the campaign, probably using something like Mosaic, which we did try to use. It was hit and miss, with some excellent Yes results in unexpected areas, but some poor ones too. In any event, this canvassing turned up when we'd already been active on the doors for 12 months and figured out our own demographics and targeting through local knowledge and research.

The challenge of canvassing wasn't just finding the voters were out, it was dealing with the seemingly endless issues that the referendum generated. Sometimes the voters just asked about something they'd seen on the TV or in the newspapers – sometimes to the extent of parroting that 'there were too many unanswered questions'. Though, this simply demonstrated the effectiveness of some of Better Together's attack lines. In any case, doorstep topics were wide – currency, childcare, university research funding, who would collect tax in Scotland, immigration, welfare, the banks, the state of the economy, etc. Defence seldom came up but lots of generalities about independence did – how would it work? So, there was a lot of explaining about devolution – what Scotland already governed – and what was left to transfer from Westminster through negotiations, the nuts and bolts of tax and administration, etc. We used positive messages and negative messages and voters asked both positive and negative questions. The idea was to talk them up the 1-10 scale and we did manage to convert a lot of undecideds to Yes. However, into 2014 itself the referendum was less a simple Yes versus No, as the Better Together parties cleverly launched (or relaunched in the case of the Liberal Democrats) individual plans for more devolved powers for Scotland. This was a clear lure to undecideds and soft Yes voters that No did not mean No. It was a predictable tactic and a reasonably effectively one as it sent out a message that the Union was reformable. The details of the proposals didn't matter too much – which helped as the Labour proposals were long, unreadable and imcomprehensible: listening to Johann Lamont trying to explain the party's income tax powers in detail was painful. But, the detail was not the point, just the simple message that voting No would deliver more devolution.

Yes Stirling University campaigners from the SSP and SNP in 2013.

6

The Things I Didn't Do

As campaigning is an immersive activity, you can get lost in it and after some time, you realize it has taken over your life. When I moved back to Edinburgh in October 2012, I had no intention of campaigning and had no idea what I was going to be involved in. Having lived in and around Stirling for years, moving back to Edinburgh was an opportunity to do different things in a much bigger city. A greater variety of galleries, cinemas, music venues, pubs etc. beckoned. So, it was a reluctant goodbye to Stirling Albion football and Stirling County rugby and the regular visits to the MacRobert Arts Centre to see the pictures. I remember going to see the film *Midnight's Children* at the Edinburgh Filmhouse in December 2012 – based on the Salman Rushdie novel about two children born at midnight on the day of Indian independence in 1948 and then secretly swapped to live very different lives in three different countries. It was a fascinating film to see knowing that the Scottish independence referendum created the possibility of our own midnight children. But, what I didn't know, was that this would be the last time I got to the cinema in Edinburgh until after the 18th September 2014. I managed to swap Stirling County for Edinburgh Rugby for a while, but this was a far from satisfactory experience in terms of entertainment. With football, I had occasional opportunities to see my eldest nephew playing for Leith Athletic and my youngest niece playing for Hibs Ladies. However, squeezing in football alongside campaigning became more difficult. Holidays also became subject to rationing. Sure enough, there was the big trip to visit university friends in Australia at the start of 2013 and a summer trip to the South of France. But 2014 was very different. In this year, holiday days were saved up for campaigning. I did take some 'real' holidays in order to avoid contracting campaign madness as we approached the big day but most of my holiday days were saved up and spent campaigning – in Drumbrae, Drylaw, Forrester Park and Muirhouse.

Holidays in Muirhouse aren't for everyone I realise, but they turned out pretty well all the same and the weather was fantastic.

At some point during the long campaign, I must have switched into constant activism though, I think, looking back, that this happened several times. In the summer of 2013, this involved relentless leafleting as well as the beginning of canvassing and public information stalls in the

An exhibit at the Yestival, Edinburgh, 12th July 2014.

evenings and at weekends. Canvassing ran in the evenings into late September, when it was getting too dark to be out round the houses. Stalls and leafleting continued, as we sought to take the case for Yes to the public on Saturday morning stalls. Leafleting was difficult, as we had already begun to deliver industrial quantities of material – meaning we were running out of stuff. I was delivering so much of the stuff myself I needed a spreadsheet to keep track. Once the Yes newspapers started to arrive, then their delivery became a constant task and we were even out delivering them between Christmas and New Year in 2013 to reach new areas (OK, I admit it, we were keen). When 2014 arrived, the campaign shifted up a gear – meaning the start of regular evening canvassing from January onwards, as well as on Saturday mornings from the Yes stall. Into summer, campaigning intensified again and became full-time in places all the way to the big day itself. How we all coped with it I'll never know, as the campaign was incredibly long and wearing by the end.

Now, whilst my experience of the campaign was a happy one in many ways – I had gainful employment at university and lots of ways to collect material for the archive and future academic projects – other people were in a different position. Take two of my fellow Yes campaigners Kate Higgins and Jenny Lindsay. Each made personal sacrifices at the referendum. Kate took a 3 month sabbatical off work and lived off of a savings plan she cashed in – instead of using it on a new kitchen as

A Yes Scotland poster in Corstorphine, Edinburgh.

intended. She became a full-time campaigner, doing canvassing morning, afternoon and evening and helping to coordinate Women for Independence activities and speaking at public meetings as often as possible. She did lots of voter registration work at colleges and bingo halls and also ran the Yes GOTV in Muirhouse on referendum day from the caravan. She also arranged the Muirhouse and Drylaw Mini Aye Festival on Saturday 13th September – a huge job in itself. Jenny Lindsay gave up her teaching job in May 2014 and lived off of savings whilst acting as events coordinator for National Collective, putting together the Yestival programme, spending hours online and on the phones ensuring Yestival and National Collective functioned in the key months leading up to September. So, she stopped earning money and also stopped doing her own art – meaning writing and poetry – and worked 24/7 on the campaign.[8] This is what the referendum did to people and also what people did with the referendum. It took over peoples' lives completely at some stage.

Finally, despite collecting and participating in the referendum, I also missed large parts of it. Because you are juggling work, campaigning and archiving, you actually miss whole chunks of the referendum campaign because you're out on the doors or sitting at the laptop creating canvassing runs and emailing/promoting campaign activities. Lots of the media coverage, events and some of the debates just passed me by. Fellow campaigners – mostly the retired – would ask me if I'd seen or heard some referendum news story and I'd just look at them blankly. Running part of the campaign was very time-intensive, often meaning there wasn't much time for anything else – like having a life and following the campaign. That was one of the ironies of the referendum. On one level I was immersed in it. But, on another level, I had no time to follow it closely at all.

7

Yes at the Centre Versus Yes on the Ground

Ross Colquhoun of the National Collective on #YesBecause day, Edinburgh, 21st August 2014.

As an organization, Yes Scotland were always with us and yet, at the same time, they weren't. I'd been to their office in Hope Street only a handful of times, once for an early campaign ideas meeting with Yes Stirling, once for the official launch of the Hope Street office and a couple of times thereafter. There were emails, some phone calls and a range of briefings but for the most part, we were on our own as a campaign group. In terms of themes, ideas, events, communities and groups and social media, Yes Scotland were good. But in terms of guidance, materials and support, they were weak. Lack of staff and office management created large holes in our knowledge and expectations of the campaign and we were left to fill them. Take two simple examples. The voter database Yesmo was basic and filled with glitches. We couldn't

Yes Scotland leaflet, January 2013.

Yes Scotland's Stephen Noon at the Yes stall on Calton Hill during the second March for Scottish Independence, 21st September 2013.

Yes Scotland Chair, Denis Canavan, addressing the marchers, 21ˢᵗ September 2013.

use it for mailshots or targeting using social marketing tools like Mosaic. It helped us find the undecideds and manage our GOTV activities come referendum day, but that was it, it was a fairly blunt instrument. Second, where it might have been useful is in voter conversion. Conversion of undecided voters was supposed to be undertaken by Yes Scotland centrally and God knows, we'd found undecideds to target. But, for whatever reason, lack of money, lack of capacity, Yes Scotland didn't do this. Moreover, this fact was

The National Collective stall at Yestival, Summerhall, Edinburgh, 12ᵗʰ July 2014.

communicated very late in the summer of 2014 so we were left revisiting the undecideds ourselves. In itself, this was no bad thing, but it was symptomatic of Yes. The centre struggled to deliver but wouldn't tell you, so we were left picking up the pieces as we ended up revisiting the undecideds not branching out into new areas.

Relying on them for anything was risky and made more problematic by the fact that some activists were used to political hierarchies – meaning people who could tell them what to do. I don't mean this in a disparaging way – what I mean is that they were used to working in an effective organization, with rules, support mechanisms and established practices. We, by contrast, were making it up as we went along and adopting a DIY approach to the campaign – it led us to solve problems ourselves rather than rely on an underpowered Hope Street. Part of what you saw

The Business for Scotland battle bus outside St. Mary's Cathedral, Leith Walk, Edinburgh, 18th August 2014.

'Dancing Darling' at the National Collective stall during the Yes Edinburgh Super Saturday, 6th September 2014.

during the referendum campaign and after is reflective of this DIY reality as campaigners learned how to be campaigners or skilled professionals in IT, marketing, social media, design etc., began to use their skills for referendum campaigning. We had a core organizational group in Edinburgh West who divided up the local workload of running stalls, canvassing, organizing public meetings, leafleting and materials and working on the referendum day organization: this latter aspect was vital as we attempted to ensure our 'missing million' voters came out to vote.

In many ways, what we did as referendum campaigners was very traditional and distinctly old school. Sure enough, we had Facebook and Twitter and one activist even ran a short instagram campaign but face-to-face contact and leafleting were really our things. We shared all the Yes Scotland infographics, with many from the artist and designer Stewart Bremner proving popular (see Bremner 2015 for a huge collection of his referendum infographics), material from the different Yes groups and new social media outlets and built a community through technology. We used Yes Scotland's Nationbuilder database to host and promote events and its database of signatories and weekly email campaign

A Vote Yes poster at the Yes Leith shop on Easter Road, Edinburgh.

blasts helped, but we also did a lot of the promotion ourselves. We promoted our campaigning activities, campaign events, voter registration, Yes Super Saturdays, etc, via social media but our real work involved doorstep canvassing, weekly information stalls, phone canvassing and some public meetings. We wanted to find supporters and undecideds and generally engage as many people as possible in a conversation about independence. Basically, we needed to change minds about independence, to get voters to understand the issue and at least consider it seriously during the campaign rather than dismiss it out of hand: this was the first time ever Scots voters had had to consider the issue in a serious way so it had a certain novelty.

8

Crowdfunding Yes

Yes Scotland was not a particularly effective organization at raising money. Without the Weirs, the Euromillions lottery winners who donated huge sums, Yes Scotland would have struggled even more than it did as a central organization. The lack of money effected everything that Yes Scotland did or didn't do – meaning campaigning materials, campaigning

The March for Scottish Independence, Edinburgh, 22nd September 2012.

itself and also the conversion of undecided voters mentioned above. And this all effected grassroots campaigning badly. However, the other side of Yes – the grassroots and the emergent national groups like National Collective and Radical Independence – were also active in fundraising and a lot of what Yes did came from the grassroots and crowdfunding efforts. Now, I admit I'd heard of crowdfunding and platforms like kickstarter before the referendum but associated them purely with small businesses and efforts to raise investment capital in a marketplace in which banks had given up lending to small businesses after the Great Financial Crisis of 2008. However, the referendum changed all that. Most Yes groups could not rely on big donors to fund their activities. They were run by volunteers and those volunteers sought to use crowdfunding platforms plus social media to generate interest and resources for their activities. And, as became clear as 2014 progressed, everyone was trying to use crowdfunding for activities large and small.

Yes artwork on display at the Aye Inspired exhibition during the Yestival, Edinburgh, 12th July 2014.

ational Collective photographic exhibition at the Yestival, Edinburgh.

Every month I think I participated in a crowdfunding venture. It had the double benefit of funding Yes activity and also producing material for the archive – which is where the Radical Independence badges, Women for Independence t-shirt, Greg Moodie cartoon book and *Scotland Yet* DVD and movie poster came from. If I'm honest, I can't remember all the stuff I crowdfunded though I did get a reminder when Indigogo's customer survey kept being emailed to me in 2015 for different campaigns I'd supported. National Collective was part of that in addition to Common Weal, *Greg Moodie versus the Union*, Generation Yes and my local Yes group. I also helped to crowdfund Yestival through National Collective's own platform. And, yes there might have been others. It was a fascinating grassroots way to fund politics – with lots of small donations via platforms promoted through social media. The practice continued after the referendum too as Newsnet Scotland, Bella

David Greig introducing the performers at his fringe show, All Back to Bowie's, on 'The Stand in the Square' during the Edinburgh Festival, 7th August 2014.

Caledonia and the Common Weal sought crowdfunding to expand their activities. The referendum had helped boost the finances and profiles of a pro-independence media and civic space and, this continued to grow after the big day itself too.

Besides crowdfunding, most of the Yes activists were also effectively funding their own campaigning. You can understand this in terms of shoe leather, transport costs and phone bills and for some of us printer cartridges and paper. Indeed, Epson was one of the big winners of the campaign from my perspective. How much we all spent on the campaign, as well as how much money we could have made by doing something completely different is not something to dwell upon, but anyone involved in political campaigning will know it swallows up time and money: unless you're a paid member of the political class and even then, it swallows up their time, money and life. The length of the referendum campaign made the demands on people quite strenuous, especially as Yes fought a very long campaign indeed. Better Together by contrast fought a long war in the media but a shorter campaign on the ground – but they could afford to as they were winning.

Yes also became something of a cottage industry both during and after the referendum. One of our activists produced Yes car decals and Yes mugs and this level of inventiveness was repeated across Scotland with t-shirts, cartoons, postcards, posters, etc. The online Yes Scotland shop certainly made money during the campaign but then lots of others raised campaign funds through their activities and some have continued, with Yes shops and products still available: look at the Free Space gallery on Easter Road in Edinburgh and you'll find Yes has continued as an exhibition space, with lots of Yes products on sale, especially from the People's Republic of Leith. Other shops and Yes organisations have continued after the referendum – not all morphing into the SNP – and so have the Yes networks and communities too.

9

Gillian Duffy Meets Eleanor Rigby

Y ou might remember Gillian Duffy from the 2010 UK general election. She was propelled to prominence after a televised campaign encounter with Labour Prime Minister Gordon Brown in Rochdale.[9] Mrs Duffy asked Brown about immigration – a sore spot for Labour as it turned out – asking him the question 'where have all these East Europeans come from?'. The problem wasn't the encounter or Brown's answer. Rather that when he returned to his car he was still being recorded live on a microphone from Sky News. When he discussed meeting Mrs Duffy with an aide in the car, his complaint that she was just 'a bigoted woman' was recorded and played on BBC Radio 2. The event sent Brown and

The National Collective stall at the Yes Edinburgh Super Saturday, 6th September 2014.

Nicola Sturgeon speaking to press at A Night for Scotland, Usher Hall, Edinburgh, 14ᵗʰ September 2014.

Labour's campaign into a tailspin. Mrs Duffy was notable because she was a lifelong Labour voter who was delivering a message that Labour didn't want to hear. It left the PM and the party appearing out of touch and also exposed Brown being nice in public and nasty in private about one of his own supporters. Indeed, Labour has struggled with this issue ever since, evident in the fact that immigration controls ended up on the Edstone of key Labour pledges in 2015, as well as on a mug sold by the party's online shop (yes, we did acquire one for the archive).

Now, frankly, we met a fair number of Gillian Duffys during the referendum, particularly in 2014. It was a problem too as we were pro-EU and pro-immigration. Immigration from other EU countries was a live issue and it was no surprise that UKIP actually had its sole electoral success in Scotland at the 2014 European election. In essence, we met UKIP's voters and it was not amongst the Guardian-reading liberals like myself, but amongst traditional Labour supporters in working class areas of Edinburgh. They were usually about Gillian Duffy's age and demographic too and it was a bit of a facet of daytime canvassing on weekdays that you'd meet voters keen to express concerns about East European immigration as EU migration increased.[10] It was a live issue

The March for Scottish Independence, Edinburgh, 22ⁿᵈ September 2012.

all right, even if the voters seemed to think that Poles didn't work and had cornered all the council housing in Edinburgh when they were actually living in expensive private rented accommodation and were all working and paying taxes: a subsequent National Records of Scotland survey found the Poles were actually the most economically active in Scotland. Read that again out loud – not the most active migrant group, the most active group in the population as a whole (The Herald, 21ˢᵗ August 2015: 4). But, to anyone with eyes to see, Edinburgh had attracted considerable numbers of new EU migrants and some voters did not see any positives in this: they saw its effects on housing, employment and culture/identity. The employment market was much more competitive and housing was expensive: nice if you're at the top, not so nice if you're at the bottom. Due to the strong Edinburgh job market as well as the economic collapse in some EU states, new generations of EU migrants had moved to the city. STV estimated that 25,000 Spanish citizens had relocated to Edinburgh in recent years.[11] The number of young, highly

James Robertson (centre) with Neal Ascherson (to his left) speaking at the Bus Party, Waterstones Falkirk, 29th May 2014.

educated Spanish workers I met over the last few years working in hotels, bars and supermarkets is one illustration of that – including qualified teachers, people with undergraduate and postgraduate qualifications and several languages, cast out by their government's austerity policies at home and unlikely to return any time soon. They will be a huge loss to a future Spain and exacerbate its difficulties with an aging society, smaller working age population plus depopulation in some areas.

The voters who mentioned immigration were generally the retired, not the 'left behinds' associated with UKIP support in Ford and Goodwin's (2014) excellent book on UKIP, *Revolt on the Right*. This book was one of the most readable academic books of 2014 and, covered the UKIP surge in support bang on time. It was part of my holiday reading in 2014, ironically in Lithuania. The thing about the research in the book is that it identified two streams of support for UKIP – defecting Conservatives in the South of England, which would certainly limit UKIP's prospects North of the border – but also a newer stand of disgruntled Labour voters that UKIP's Deputy Chairman Paul Nuttall MEP sought to cultivate in the North of England. Now, you can see why that was a potentially big problem for Yes at the referendum – as we promoted EU membership,

The Project Wish tree, Yestival, Edinburgh, 12th July 2014.

immigration and welfare – and for the SNP and Labour in Scotland as UKIP positioned itself to attract their voters. However, whilst UKIP managed to elect one MEP in 2014 (with 140,534 votes and 10.5%) its success vanished in Scotland come 2015. UKIP managed 3,881,099 votes across the UK at the general election, worth 12.6%. However, the Scottish performance was much less impressive, with UKIP winning just 47,078 votes and 1.6%. It lost every deposit too, so there was nothing like the result in England, where the party turned in 125 second places with 14.1% of the vote and neatly positioned itself as the main alternative to Labour in many seats in Northern England.

Concern about EU immigration was not the only reason we met quite a few Gillian Duffys. The other reason was demographic. There were several thousand more women than men in the constituency and, I'd guess there was an age imbalance here too, with more female than male pensioners: though this might just be a facet of who we talked to

A Women for Independence stall at Pennywell Road, Muirhouse, Edinburgh, 13th September 2014.

and which part of the constituency we talked to them in. Not that the constituency was atypical for Scotland in its age profile – though it did lack voters amongst the 18-24 age groups. In terms of households it contained 32.9% one person households – below the Scottish average – with 14.5% over 65, just above the average.[12]

However, despite these averages, campaigning did involve meeting a lot of elderly women voters in single households. Some clearly had limited contact with the outside world and were very much living a lonely existence. Ironically, some were alone because their families had emigrated or moved away and you often got a sense that you were the only person likely to break their isolation that day. Some of the elderly answered the door in a confused state, which meant the referendum went out the window as you spent the time checking that they were fine. It wasn't all Eleanor Rigby though. There were some great conversations to be had with pensioners about their local areas, their memories of moving there and how their families were getting on.

10

Voter Registration and the Missing Million

A view of the flats in the northern part of Muirhouse, Edinburgh.

One of the most important aspects of the referendum campaign involved voter registration. Given demographic factors, we were acutely aware that a fair section of potential Yes voters weren't on the electoral register – the young plus disengaged working class voters. A lot of grassroots campaigning sought to address this problem – part of the logic behind the mass canvasses of housing estates organized by the Radical Independence Campaign in Dundee, Edinburgh and Glasgow amongst other places. Radical Independence members came to help us canvass on Super Saturday in Drylaw and Muirhouse as well as on a later canvass in Drumbrae. Thankfully, there was a postponement of UK efforts to reform electoral registration before the 2014 referendum. The new scheme to replace the role of a head of household registering all voters in the property with individual electoral registration was likely to depress registration, turnout and the Yes vote had it been adopted in 2014. Postponement of the new measure meant electoral registration did not get any worse, but that didn't mean it would get any better either. Therefore, it became a constant focus of grassroots efforts as we sought to register as many voters as possible.

Martello Court in Muirhouse, Edinburgh.

Willie Sullivan's study *The Missing Scotland* estimated that over one million Scots were absent from electoral democracy – either through remaining unregistered or through being registered but resisting party efforts to get them to participate at all. Electoral turnout across the UK had been a problem for several decades, as had declining party memberships: though this seems to have gone into reverse since the referendum and the UK general election of 2015. UK turnout reached its nadir at the 2001 general election when it fell 11.9% to 59.4%: the lowest turnout since 1918. This development sparked some experiments to increase turnout like all-postal voting, electronic voting, etc. Though devolution created a number of devices to increase political engagement through the petitions process, the parliamentary education service, Holyrood moving outside Edinburgh and publishing its materials online, electoral turnout was a disappointment. Holyrood turnout had peaked at 58% at the first Holyrood election in 1999, dipping beneath 50% in 2003 and then sitting at 50.4% in 2011: which is sobering when you realise this was the election that gave birth to the independence referendum. Turnout at local elections and European elections were even worse. The Scottish local elections

Messages from the Project Wish Tree, Yestival, 12th July 2014.

of 2012 saw a turnout of 39.1% and the 2014 European election was even smaller at 33.5%. And, rather than think about national results, the way to interpret turnout is at the local level – in Edinburgh's Forth ward, which contained Muirhouse, Pilton and Royston Mains, turnout was a below average 37.8 per cent in 2012. Multimember wards make it difficult to determine turnout but the surrounding wards saw higher turnout: Almond to the West registered 44.3 per cent turnout, whilst Inverleith to the South saw 47.9 per cent turnout. It didn't help that Muirhouse was also shrinking through demolition of flats and population displacement at the time.

Though Edinburgh City Council worked to register voters through its annual canvass, plenty of voters had slipped through the net for one reason or another. Some of this was political – people were disenchanted with politics, politicians, political parties and institutions. They stopped voting, fell off of the electoral register and had a healthy disdain for the political establishment (which was fiddling its parliamentary expenses and getting us to pay to have their moats cleaned). Focus group research by IPSOS-Mori for Sullivan's book found that non-voters were not disinterested in politics or their communities, rather that they thought

New Muirhouse - the flats and houses being built on Pennywell Road, Muirhouse Edinburgh in 2015-16.

voting wouldn't make a difference, that the parties were all too similar, that politicians were not trusted and that there was a lack of information on where and how to vote (Sullivan 2014: 21). When you replay the last decade of politics in the UK you can understand some of the reasons here – parties competing for the centre ground and becoming less distinctive, the rise of professional politicians and the Westminster elite from private schools and Oxbridge, the various MP's expenses scandals and a general rise in distrust of institutions. Throw in economic crisis, banking scandals, austerity, the widening gap between the rich and the poor and you realize there has clearly been a lot to put people off politics as well as voting.

However, there were also more practical reasons for people to be missing from the register. Some people were hiding to avoid debt repayments. Not the poll tax debts, but more recent debts to people like loan sharks. And, some people were worried about being found too so took no chances and stayed off of the register at the referendum: we had quite a few conversations with residents about this, who were genuinely worried about what might happen if they registered. Others had fallen

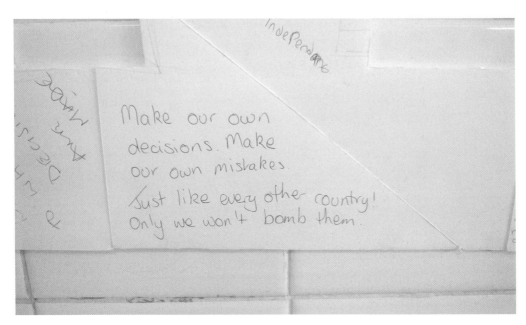

The Independence Jigsaw at the Muirhouse Community Shop, 3rd September 2014.

Yes Edinburgh West campaigning in Drylaw in 2014.

A Yes cake at the Yes Edinburgh Super Saturday in Leith, 2nd August 2014.

off the register through literacy problems, being unable to keep track of the various registration forms and understand the paperwork. One of the most basic things we did with people was explain how voting worked and how to handle the application – giving them the forms and envelopes and explaining the mechanics of voting, the what, where and when. In short, we needed to give people the support and confidence to exercise their rights as citizens. I can't emphasise enough how important that was, both to the campaign and to democracy in general. Also, there was a constant churn of people moving through Edinburgh's large private rented sector: a sector which extended way beyond the flats of Dalry, Gorgie and Leith to the suburbs in some numbers. Did I expect to find a private rental markct out in Drumbrae and Muirhouse? No, but that market is there, even in places you least expect it and the movement of people renting across Edinburgh made for lots of unregistered voters.

Finally, if you wonder why politicians and commentators mention the level of public engagement at the referendum as a unique thing, the high turnout and level of electoral registrations are part of the reason. And, it wasn't simply the case of getting people to fill out forms. Public

Yes Edinburgh activists at their Super Saturday event in Leith, 2nd August 2014.

engagement meant you were helping to enfranchise people in some of Scotland's most disadvantaged communities, promoting active citizenship and democracy and explaining how the political system operated. We might have been some of the only people who came to talk about politics with them as parties had abandoned low turnout areas. This type of public engagement had an educational impact on them and us. A lot of the doorstep campaigning involved conversations about how devolution operated, what local councils were responsible for as well as Westminster policies and practices. But we also listened to the problems and choices that faced local communities, families and individuals in relation to major questions as well as their daily lives.

11
Breakfast at Gerry's

Gerry's café sits at the end of the Pennywell Road shops, just before the Gunner pub. Gerry's is a café by day and a chip shop by night. A day of campaigning in Muirhouse would usually begin at Gerry's, with cappuccino and a bacon roll and, for some, as full a cooked breakfast as was possible. For lunch it would be the North Edinburgh Arts Centre where you had to get in early to avoid disappointment – especially on days when curry was on the menu. A small group of us lived off of the food in these two places on and off for weeks and they became our informal campaign bases in the months leading up to the referendum. Yes Edinburgh West held our own Super Saturday event in

Michael Stewart supporting the Yes Edinburgh West Mini-Aye festival in Muirhouse, 13th September 2014.

The 'Aye or Naw' window at the Muirhouse Community Shop, 3rd September 2014.

Muirhouse and Drylaw, with stalls, canvassing, leafleting and between that, continuous campaigning and the Aye festival on 13th September we must have given a mini economic stimulus to the Muirhouse economy during the long campaign: at the cafes, shops and Greggs.

The reason we spent so much time in Muirhouse was simple – it was full of potential Yes voters but also experienced low levels of voter registration and turnout: the missing million discussed above. It was a priority area for us. Initially, there wasn't a great deal of enthusiasm amongst our campaigners about going to Muirhouse – the area had a reputation for non-voting and social problems after all. It had a starring role in Irvine Welsh's *Trainspotting* as early as page 16, when Renton sought to score some drugs off of Mike Forrester in one of the Muirhouse flats – probably Inchmickery Court from the description in the book, with its unusual five storey maisonettes. This part of *Trainspotting* also featured Renton's infamous visit to the toilet in the betting shop at the Pennywell Arcade: though now he'd have a choice of Ladbrokes and William Hill.

After holding one stall in the area at the Pennywell Arcade shops the campaigners were converted to working in the area following the excellent reception from local people. Basically, you can't go to Muirhouse without

The Independence Choir at Yes Edinburgh West's Mini-Aye festival, Muirhouse, 13th September 2014.

falling over Yes supporters – either from the estate itself or from West Pilton across the road. We canvassed part of the area in the summer of 2013 and were back in 2014, with some permanent canvassing, meaning doing it morning, afternoon and evening, day after day as we worked our way from houses to flats and back again as we became a permanent presence in the area.

The geography of Muirhouse is a changing one. In essence, it's a community that is being demolished and rebuilt, simultaneously, bit by bit. When we first went leafleting there, some of the streets we went to leaflet no longer existed – the houses were gone and some of the area was grassed over but they still appeared on the electoral register. Some of the small blocks of flats in mid-Muirhouse had gone and the one or two that were left were empty and derelict, though we had to check whether the flats were completely unoccupied. Since we started campaigning there, parts of Muirhouse and West Pilton have been building sites, with the former site of Craigroyston High School going from a gap site to a bustling area of new houses from 2014-5.

The way to understand Muirhouse is to explain it area by area. The southern-most part off of Ferry Road has new flats and townhouses at Ferrygait; a rebuilt Muirhouse Green of flats and houses for families, with little streets full of kids playing; an area of semi-vacant land between the Green and Pennywell Road that formerly held Craigroyston High School and was to become new housing built by Urban Union in 2014-15.[13] Middle Muirhouse had a mix of traditional council flats and lots of new housing, whilst the northernmost part of Muirhouse had flats and maisonettes in blocks of flats, as well as the former terror tower itself, Martello Court (which is now very different). North of the high flats and across Muirhouse Parkway, was the small community of Salvesen: an area of postwar veterans housing created by the former Salvesen whaling company.

Salvesen is a fascinating example of post-war social history. The company was founded in 1872 by a Norwegian immigrant. It began as a firm of shipping agents in Leith, then moved into whaling, trawlers and then commercial transport – I can remember seeing its lorry fleet on Scotland's roads and motorways with its distinctive Norwegian flag logo, before it was taken over by another transport company, Norbert Dentressangle. After the second world war, Salvesen and a range of other organisations funded veterans housing in the area. The housing was built by the Scottish Veterans Garden City Association (founded in 1915), which explains the garden city type of housing in the area: influenced by Ebenezer Howard and generating a housing movement across the UK. If you've ever been to Welwyn Garden City or Port Sunlight on Merseyside you'll get the picture. And they are still adding housing units now, to provide support to more recent veterans. When you walk around the area you see lots of the homes were funded or sponsored by companies and associations: with little plaques from organisations like the Scottish Motor Traction Company, RAF Benevolent Fund, Henry Robb Shipbuilders, Edinburgh Charities Day Committee, Red Cross Association, Distillers Company, Henry Wells and Co., Scottish Woollen Comforts Council, etc. The houses were built in the immediate post-war period, with Salvesen Gardens opened in 1948 for military veterans, along with Salvesen Terrace and Gardens. Salvesen Crescent opened in 1948 for retired lighthouse keepers and Salvesen Grove was added in 1950. And, though this was 1940s housing from a conflict that ended in 1945, we still met veterans there in 2013 and 2014 from more recent conflicts: some were Yes, some were No.

Whilst Salvesen owed its street names to whaling and philanthropy, parts of Muirhouse owed their names to the Forth. All of the flats in

Salveson Gardens, Edinburgh.

the Northern part of Muirhouse had their origins on sea or shore along the River Forth. Inchmickery Court was named after an island in the Forth estuary, which is effectively directly North of Muirhouse itself. May Court was named after the Isle of May, an island and bird sanctuary in the Forth on the way to the North Sea. Fidra Court was named after an island off of North Berwick to the East of Edinburgh. Gunnet Court was named after a rock or ledge in the Forth, between Inchcolm and Inchkeith, North of Leith. The infamous Martello Court was named after an actual Martello tower in Leith docks, as well as the rocks off of the tower itself. The Martello towers were created as defensive fortifications during the Napoleonic wars, and the one at Leith was one of three in Scotland, though these structures were built all around the world. Finally, Oxcars Court was named after a lighthouse in the Forth, situated between Inchcolm and Inchmickery islands and Birnie Court was named after a group of rocks in the Forth North of Muirhouse. The flats were where we were at our most meticulous when it came to voter registration – compiling hand written lists of voters and missing voters from various sources to determine who was on the electoral roll and who we should seek to sign up. Our voter registrations efforts in Muirhouse were continuous until the day registration closed at midnight on 2nd September 2014.

When Yes Edinburgh West hosted its own Super Saturday on 5th July 2014 we chose Muirhouse and Drylaw for the day. Super Saturday was a monthly campaign event organized by the Yes Edinburgh umbrella group. The idea was simply to have a day of campaigning each month in one of the Edinburgh constituencies, at which all the local Yes groups would combine. It created a by-election feel on the day as 200 or so campaigners from Yes, Radical Independence, Women for Independence etc. would turn up to campaign. There would be stalls, canvassing and leafleting arranged and the number of campaigners involved meant the local host group could get through a huge amount of work in a key area: something that would take them weeks to achieve normally. Super Saturday in Drylaw and Muirhouse gave us an opportunity to flood the two areas with campaigners to find and develop as much support as possible, with stalls, leafleting and canvassing. We had something like 38 canvass runs made up for the morning and got through them all, catching more voters on a Saturday morning than you usually do through evening canvassing. When you replicate that across all the different parts of Edinburgh – Craigmillar and Wester Hailes for example – you get the measure of how much grassroots campaigning was done. When you link these to election results at the UK general election in 2015 – when support for the SNP soared and Labour collapsed, you can get understanding of how politics has changed in these areas over time too.

The last Saturday before polling day was 13th September. And, as many campaigners know, the last Saturday is a key date in the electoral calendar to galvanise campaigners and voters alike. The plan for Yes Edinburgh West was to make some noise to mobilise the Yes vote in Drylaw and Muirhouse, two areas in which by that stage we'd undertaken a huge amount of work. The plan was to do everything we could all day to make sure voters would turn out on the 18th – handing out badges, posters, balloons, basically anything we could get out hands on to raise the Yes profile as much as we could in the days leading up to the vote. Given the location of the stalls, we also galvanized the Yes vote across West Pilton too. We'd be doing some of this again on the day, with our get out the vote efforts, but we started it early. Of course, this wasn't a simple piece of political campaigning – the type of things we'd been doing for months. Rather, this was the Drylaw and Muirhouse Aye Festival, organized and orchestrated by Kate Higgins and an excellent piece of political carnival. The day involved some of the normal political activities on a bigger scale – 5-6 stalls, canvassing, some leafleting – but also a Woman for Independence rally at the North Edinburgh Arts Centre, hosted by Elaine C. Smith, followed by a women's car cavalcade across Edinburgh to Craigmillar (and it had to avoid the march along Princes Street by the Orange Order). There was face painting and a nail bar, music from folk singers and the Independence Choir – which toured Muirhouse singing to the local population led by the Radical Independence banner. The choir went down to the flats and let loose and people came out onto their balconies to watch the spectacle. We had speaker vans featuring music and political messages – including several tours by Colin Fox of the SSP – all intended to mobilise the voters and encourage them to keep their nerve. We were trying to reassure them basically. Yes Sport campaigner Michael Stewart came down to talk to voters at the Muirhouse and Drylaw stalls and had a kickabout with some of the locals too. Some of our campaigners were puzzled about why we were saturating a couple of areas we had worked in beyond saturation point. However, when you've spent a year and a half registering voters in one of the poorest areas of electoral turnout, you've got to keep making some noise to make sure they vote. And, on the day, in turnout terms, it worked. We had found a fair number of the missing million, registered them and many voted for the first time in their lives.

Two final things about Muirhouse. First, this is a very diverse community, with people from all around the world living there – Scots, English, Poles, Africans, Syrians, Iraqis, amongst others. It also has more than its fair share of difficulties. It has parts of serious deprivation and some of the people here are at the sharpest end of austerity. Like lots of places, it has problem housing, crime, drugs, unemployment, etc. Unfortunately, it's probably known for these issues more than anything. But, with the right support and investment it has been turning itself around.

Second, daytime canvassing was often hard going in Muirhouse from Monday to Friday. Why? Because so few people were at home. They were at work. This might surprise you but the truth is that, despite its many problems, Muirhouse is on the up. Its housing and population are growing again. It continues to face a host of social and economic problems but has an active residents group (TRIM), has community facilities like the library, North Edinburgh Arts Centre, Community Shop and Millennium Centre and a lot of local social and educational activities too. It has a new secondary school, new housing and is getting a lot of targeted investment in housing and health – with the Scottish Government adding the local primary school, Craigroyston, to its attainment challenge programme in 2015.

A Yes Rally at George Square, Glasgow, 16th September 2014. (Image courtesy of Cameron Pow)

12

Drumbrae – Walking Through Childhood

One of the most striking things to observe locally in Edinburgh Western was the extent of social change in Drumbrae. In my childhood, Drumbrae was the council housing estate next to my primary school, Foxcovert (which comprised a RC and non-denominational schools sharing a campus way before such things became fashionable),

Essendean Place in Drumbrae, Edinburgh.

where lots of my schoolmates lived. But since Mrs Thatcher and council house sales in the 1980s, there were now a lot of homeowners and people renting from the private rented sector, in both the houses and the flats. How much council stock was left was hard to see. But, what I did notice was that almost everyone who had lived there in my schooldays seemed to have gone – to be replaced by a churn of residents through the private rented sector. Drumbrae primary school had gone, replaced by an old folk's home and my old primary Fox Covert had shrunk in size drastically. In its heyday of the postwar baby boom, Fox Covert had over 20 huts as extra classrooms as well as a building extension on one side. Now, the only block of huts left was the daycare centre. Part of the school's playing fields in the 1970s had been sold off to create Queen Margaret College and that too had gone, to be replaced by new flats and houses in Clerwood.

What hadn't changed in Drumbrae was the shops, the Clermiston Inn pub (the Clerry Inn) and the street names. Whoever had designed Drumbrae back in the 1950s was a fan of Robert Louis Stevenson in general and *Kidnapped* in particular though not entirely accurate when it came to spelling. Anyone familiar with RLS and Drumbrae will get the connection – it's the kind of area that has Alan Breck Gardens for example. Some of *Kidnapped* was set locally, from the Rest And Be Thankful on Corstorphine Hill at the end of the book, to Cramond and the Hawes Inn at South Queensferry, so it isn't hard to see why the council decided to recognize the local connection through naming streets in the estate. However, just about every street in Drumbrae has a *Kidnapped* connection – Essendean Place (the fictional town in the Borders where Balfour lived), Hoseason Gardens (after Captain Elias Hoseason of the Covenanter), Ransome Gardens (after the ship's cabin boy, Ransome), Torrance Park (after the lawyer's assistant) plus a host of streets named after geographical locations and clan names in *Kidnapped* like Duart Crescent, Morven Street, Balfron Loan, Ardsheil Avenue, Glenure Loan, Rannoch Road, Dochart Drive and the misspelt Durar Drive (which is Duror in the book). Why these names were picked and not others – like the main character David Balfour[14] – we don't know, but the geography of his travels mark Drumbrae very clearly.[15]

Drumbrae itself was an important area for the Yes campaign as it contained exactly the kind of voters we were targeting – Labour voters. Sure enough, it had SNP and Liberal Democrat voters, but Drumbrae was

Hoseason Gardens, Drumbrae, Edinburgh.

one of the few areas of Edinburgh Western that had a Labour councillor and the electorate of Drumbrae was part of the reason for that. Given demographics in the constituency and the political content of the Yes campaign, targeting Labour voters in this area was vital – if we couldn't make progress here, we would lose and lose badly. So, Drumbrae became a major locus of our campaigning, as we sought to persuade voters up the 1-10 scale, convert undecideds and generally maintain our support over two summers. We started there early in the summer of 2013 and worked our way up and down the houses and flats through 2014 to the referendum. Days would begin over coffee at the Drumbrae hub and we steadily covered and recovered the area through individual and group canvassing plus help from Radical Independence campaigners. Bit by bit we built support in the area, though some of this probably slipped back in the latter stages of the campaign as the Vow, Gordon Brown's campaigning, mailshots and the *Daily Record* appealed to Labour supporters to vote No

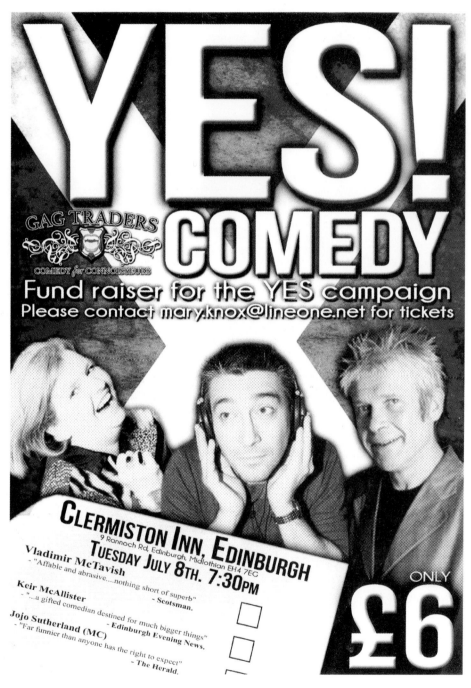

The poster for the Yes Edinburgh West 'Comedy Night' fundraiser at the Clermiston Inn, 8th July 2014.

for greater devolution. Though some Labour figures came out for Yes during the referendum we needed more – and especially more senior Labour figures to commit, but Labour held together on the issue. There were lots of Yessers in the Drumbrae area though, who encouraged us to use the Clerry Inn pub for campaigning and social events – whether it was the Friday night socials or the Yes comedy fundraiser with Vladimir McTavish, Keir McAllister and Jojo Sutherland. We established this early on by chance, much as we established that lots of local men didn't like Alex Salmond or Heart of Midlothian football club and they usually told us this forcefully: who knew Drumbrae was full of Labour voting, Hibs fans? One of these voters asked us innocently if we were being paid to campaign and seemed sure we were from some business organization far away rather than living locally and campaigning as volunteers. It does give you an insight into what voters think about the politically active though: we're not just geeks from outer space, but paid geeks.

The Spirit of Independence fire engine at the Yes Edinburgh Super Saturday, 6th September 2014.

13

18th September 2014 – The Beginning, Not the End?

When the 18ᵗʰ September finally came, I was already tired and set for a long day and night. Many of our campaigners were up before the crack of dawn to deliver Yes A-boards to all our polling stations as well as attending the opening of the polling stations and boxes. I wasn't one of them. Instead I was up early to make it to Stirling University for my first politics lecture at 9am – 250 new students about to listen to a lecture on British politics on the day it was set to change, one way or another. It was a murky day, with mist across central Scotland, which didn't clear until the afternoon. Because I had a postal vote, my vote was

Yes campaigners getting out the vote in Muirhouse, on referendum day, 18ᵗʰ September 2014.

already cast, posted and verified and doubtless studied closely by Scottish Conservative leader Ruth Davidson.[16] When the ballot paper appeared in the post, I opened it then sat looking at it, completely overwhelmed. It was just a bit of paper, but then I never thought I'd ever get the chance to vote at an independence referendum. I realized I was completely unable to fill it in alone so went up to my parents to vote Yes with them in the home I grew up in. They were rather bemused by this of course.

After a day of teaching and meeting with students it was back to Edinburgh to help with get out the vote. We'd split the constituency into four, with an emphasis on doing the maximum amount of work in the areas of poorest turnout, in which the Yes vote was likely to be highest.

Yes activists at the polling station at Kelvindale, Glasgow, 18th September 2014. (Image courtesy of Cameron Pow).

The various GOTV coordinators on the day worked away steadily with the campaign workers on the ground and our vote turned out, without us really having to coax them. The Muirhouse GOTV was run by Kate Higgins from a temporary caravan adjacent to one of the area's two polling stations – a very wobbly caravan, as no one had put the stabilizing legs down. Voting was steady at the polling station there all day, even so, we still went about knocking-up the Yes vote to make sure it appeared. There was also a carnival atmosphere in the area, with home made banners, posters, flags hanging from flat balconies, etc. We also created some ourselves by arranging for a bagpiper to lead a parade of Yessers through the streets as a voting reminder – an idea stolen from Yes Craigmillar. GOTV in Muirhouse was then followed by transferring to nearby Drylaw, which involved working through the evening with handwritten lists of Yes voters compiled after the Yesmo database had closed. Aided by a group of campaigners from Radical Independence we completed the last of the GOTV in the dark. Voters were still coming to the polling station at 9.45 too. However, once that was completed it was off to the count at Ingliston, which was not a happy affair given the result and the fact that the loss of Clackmannanshire so early gave us a pretty clear indication that it would not be our night.

A lot of our campaigners were new. They'd never been to a count before. They'd also never seen much of the opposition before during the campaign. We'd tried to get on with our own campaign rather than worry about what Better Together was up to. Mostly, they had relied on direct mail with a limited amount of doorstep work from what we could see. However, the individual parties themselves – Conservative, Labour and Liberal Democrat – had done a fair bit of canvassing, combining electioneering with the referendum: Labour and the Lib Dems were active trying to contest the Westminster seat in advance of the 2015 general election. Labour had also been active doing phone canvassing.

The Yes caravan in Muirhouse on referendum day.

The count was the first time we saw them in the flesh and, this being Edinburgh, there was a lot of them as they had galvanized their supporters and activists in the latter stages of the campaign (the Sunday Times poll that gave Yes the lead doubtless helped here): and many were from a version of Edinburgh we had seldom encountered.[17] When it came to observing the count, our main aim was to figure out how well we'd done across our different polling stations to see if our vote had turned out and held up and mostly it did. It was, however, dwarfed by the No vote. Edinburgh voted No by 61.1% to 38.9%. In Edinburgh West it was 65.5% No to 34.5% Yes: 22,615 people voted Yes, compared to 42,946 No. The closest Edinburgh contest was in East, where Yes polled 47%, but in general, Edinburgh was a disappointment, albeit a predictable one. There were local areas we had won across the 5 Edinburgh counting areas (which were the Westminster parliamentary constituencies) but,

The count in Stirling, 18th September 2014.

our results, plus the lack of Yes results across the rest of Scotland made for a bad night.

Apart from one brief moment when I thought we might actually win the referendum – the morning of the Sunday Times poll of 7th September 2014 that gave Yes a two point lead – I'd expected to lose. So, referendum night itself did not come as a shock. Occasional poll evidence or doorstep results would provide some encouragement as we felt we were gaining momentum. However, in Edinburgh generally, it was hard to see how a Yes vote could be delivered outwith some local communities. In essence, our campaign was really about increasing the Yes vote to counteract the huge Edinburgh No. We needed other parts of Scotland to deliver a Yes. There was also the hope that we might overturn the No lead on turnout. Essentially, by identifying as many Yes supporters as possible – in areas like Drumbrae and Muirhouse – making sure they were registered and turned out on the day itself, we hoped we could get over the line. To some extent, we managed this. The Yes vote turned out. We had a carnival atmosphere, with lots of noise, flags and an unusually good turnout in low turnout areas. The problem was, our high turnout would be 70%, whereas a high turnout in a strong No area would be 90%. This fact became evident on the day itself and gave

The referendum count in Glasgow. (Image courtesy of Processed Beets).

Nicola Sturgeon and Humza Yousaf at the count in Glasgow. (Image courtesy of Processed Beets).

a pretty strong indication of how things were going to go. Between our campaigning and the narrowing in the opinion polls, the shy No voters had woken up and came out in droves.

The day after the referendum was a slow one. Basically, I was exhausted and took to cleaning the flat as a displacement activity. TV was hard to watch too, for obvious reasons. However, when David Cameron made his statement about the referendum outside 10 Downing Street, everything changed. Cameron's embrace of English Votes for English Laws was a masterstroke for his party, but not for the Union. His announcement completely outflanked Labour, left people like Gordon Brown looking ridiculous and gave the impression that <u>this</u> was what the referendum had been all about. Cameron's promotion of EVEL plus Osborne's skillful pursuit of devolution and a Northern powerhouse had the effect of hurting Labour and also acting as a shield against UKIP's embrace of English nationalism: it had been used extensively but unsuccessfully at the Clacton by-election. But, in Scotland, it seemed to run against all the warm, 'family of nations together' rhetoric from the campaign.

The combined effect of the referendum, the long mobilization of Yes and Cameron's support for English nationalism had a major effect on the SNP and the Greens. The fact that the referendum had radicalized and activated so many people on the Yes campaign was a positive thing. Even though the referendum ended in defeat, I did have the distinct impression these activists were not simply going to down tools and return to private life – they were going to go somewhere, though not necessarily in the huge numbers observed after 18th September. Some people in the SNP seemed to think referendum defeat would mean organizational crisis – a post-1979 scenario of membership contraction and financial crisis, which was entirely understandable but at odds with what Yes campaigners were actually thinking. The fact that the SNP, Greens and SSP all immediately increased their membership after the referendum did not surprise me. But, the scale did. SNP chief executive Peter Murrell relayed the rising number via his twitter account and the numbers rolled higher and higher with every tweet from the 19th September onwards: I know some people who joined whilst watching Cameron speaking outside Number 10. It was the same with the Greens, though in lesser numbers. The SNP's staff and computer systems could not cope with the surge and neither could the Greens: their technology was overwhelmed. Lots of people joined online, but there were also paper applications to process too. All at a time when staff were exhausted after a long referendum campaign that ended in defeat. The SSP didn't have the money to send out membership packs initially because of the new levels of interest. Given that the trend in most Western democracies was for party memberships to decline, this was a fascinating development, followed subsequently by a Green surge in England in Wales into 2015, a Liberal Democrat membership surge after the 2015 general election defeat and Labour membership growth with the UK party's leadership contest over the summer of 2015. For the Yes parties, the growth in membership transformed the post-referendum mood and also, their electoral prospects. The SNP was already well-resourced, with a strong membership before the referendum, now it became a mega-party in Scottish terms. The Greens suddenly became a party with a bigger budget, more campaigners and more staff too – all important for party development and future electoral growth.

In addition, the Yes parties took up the Vow – to ensure it was implemented in full. This gave them a clear post-referendum goal in the short-term, aided by the formation of the Smith Commission on more powers. The Commission might seem unimportant but politically, it meant that the constitutional question remained centre stage in Scottish and UK politics, rather than pushed aside after the 18th September. It

The tellers rest before the counting of the votes begins. (Image courtesy of Processed Beets).

also exposed the horse-trading over the devolution reform package, which helped the Yes parties and Scottish Government to stake out their positions and argue over the fulfillment of the vow. Despite losing the referendum, the surge in memberships plus the debate around Smith (and bitterness of some about how the referendum was lost) all provided the SNP in particular with political impetus that it took into the 2015 UK general election. Neither devolution nor the defeat of independence had killed nationalism stone dead.

14

May 2015 – Scotland Elects 56 Yes MPs

The 2015 UK general election was the first occasion at which I'd watched the election from my own home since 1992. At the independence referendum I was at the count at Ingliston, taking photographs for the Scottish Political Archive as well as observing the count for Yes Edinburgh West. Before this, almost all my election nights had involved media work, usually live, usually all-night and into the morning too, fuelled by Jelly beans and bananas. In the old days, this involved hours on end at Queen Margaret Drive in Glasgow, then more recently at Pacific Quay. Sometimes the BBC booked me a hotel room though I was seldom in it. It was really just somewhere to take a shower and change clothes.

In 1997, I'd been doing political analysis for Sky TV from the count at Meadowbank when Labour won a landslide and Conservative luminaries like Malcolm Rifkind lost his seat. In 2003, Sky had me at the Glasgow count in the SECC when the SSP won two Glasgow list seats, trying to talk down a camera live to the network whilst SSP supporters jubilantly sang the red flag behind me. Other election nights were more sedate – meaning sharing the studio with journalists and politicians at the BBC. This meant overnight with Radio 5 and John Pienaar in 2007, Derek Bateman and Radio Scotland in 2011, as well as Westminster elections and occasional by-elections. So, 2015 was very different. I was booked to do a couple of slots with Radio 5 from 6am the morning after the election, from the Elephant House café on Edinburgh's George IV Bridge, which meant I could watch election night on TV: a novel experience.

Election night on TV was dramatic at every level. The huge exit poll that the BBC led with at 10pm as the polling stations closed on election night was a stunning beginning to its coverage: so much so that politicians and pundits refused to believe it. It forecast a Conservative lead that grew during the night as it went from largest party on a forecast of 316 seats to an actual 330 seats and a clear majority. It indicated Liberal Democrat collapse (10 forecast but only 8 in reality), Labour disappointment (239 seats forecast, but only 232 at the end of the night) and a landslide for the SNP (with 58 out of 59 seats forecast, though the real result was 56 MPs). At one stage it looked like the SNP might even win Orkney and Shetland, though, it ended up being one of the three seats that eluded the SNP surge. In Dumfriesshire, Clydesdale and Tweedale, the sole Conservative MP David Mundell held off the SNP by just 798 votes, as the SNP vote grew by 27.5% compared to 2010. In Edinburgh South, a lot of tactical voting saw Labour's Ian Murray hold on. The SNP increased its vote by 26.1%, but Labour also increased its support by 4.4% and gained enough tactical votes in areas like Morningside to compensate for its collapse in areas of traditional Labour support. Still, all in all, it was an incredible night for the SNP. If you had offered anyone in the party 56 seats before the election, they'd have bitten your hand off.

The SNP surge had been highlighted in opinion polls for months on end before the May election but even then the actual results were breathtaking. On the one hand, the forecast gains were unbelievable, as they involved a remarkable change in the political weather and a catastrophic collapse of Scottish Labour in its strongest areas. On the other hand, having met so many Yessers during the referendum and realized they were bound to solidify their allegiance to the SNP, the results in Scotland were completely believable. For a lot of voters, there was no turning back to Labour or the Liberal Democrats and a lot of Yes supporters or one-off SNP voters from 2007 or 2011 became much more strongly committed to the SNP. However, it's worth remembering how poor the SNP's history at Westminster elections was until 2015. The party's sole notable victories were back in February and October 1974 and had yielded 7 and then 11 seats out of 71. Since then, the party had been an irrelevant force at Westminster elections and in the House of Commons. The party had learned to win at Scottish elections, with a narrow victory in 2007 and then a landslide in 2011. But, in between was a highly disappointing Westminster performance in 2010, at which the SNP had won only 19.9% of the vote and 6 seats out of 59. At that election the SNP won only 491,386 votes. By 2015, it had increased that by almost 1 million. Strathclyde University's John Curtice had long referred to the 'Holyrood' gap in SNP electoral support – with stronger support at lower turnout, Scottish elections that suited its policy agenda and government aspirations and much weaker support at higher turnout UK elections, that were dominated by the main British parties on their policy agendas and government prospects. However, the 2015 experience completely shattered the Holyrood gap idea, leading to what political commentator Gerry Hassan referred to as 'Peak SNP', as the party actually did much better than it had in 2011, though looked to do even better come the Scottish election in 2016.

15

ScotRef: Approach With Caution

If you have followed social media since the 18th September 2014, it won't have escaped your notice that there is a community of Yes campaigners who want to hold a second referendum as quickly as possible. Some even thought the No vote was achieved through electoral fraud and the fact that postal votes were sent South for verification. The Yes vote wasn't stolen though - it was simply a clear victory for No. Despite our efforts and message, too few people were convinced, even though we took Margo's conversion goal into multiple numbers. Most of the people I spoke to at the referendum in Edinburgh Western were No voters – I met them every week at stalls and on the doorsteps. We covered as many areas as we could in the constituency and also attended Yes Super Saturdays in other parts of Edinburgh and, with some exceptions, it was hard to see how it was going to be a Yes on the ground. Given the demographics and political complexion of Edinburgh Western, this is not surprising and, given Edinburgh generally, with its large number of professional and finance jobs and proliferation of private schools, a No vote here was pretty likely in 2014. Our task was to try to close the gap between Yes and No in our part of Edinburgh and hope that other parts of Scotland would take Yes across the winning line.

However, we didn't even get close in our area – only 22,615 people voted Yes, compared to 42,946 for No, though our support did grow on the ground during the campaign. The Yes vote did end up staying Yes, and electing a SNP MP in 2015 but we were way short at the one that mattered in 2014 (and then the SNP fell back locally in the elections in 2016 and 2017). The question therefore is, will any of this change in future to create a Yes majority and if so, when is this likely to happen? Given the very different 2016 Brexit referendum results North and South of the border there was a strong additional impetus for a second independence

The Remain ceilidh at the Scottish Parliament on 22nd June 2016.

referendum, but that doesn't mean we know if and when it will happen despite the Scottish Government's initial timetable announced in March 2017 or its post-general election reset. The post-Brexit referendum period has seen a lot of debate, process and maneuvering on the issue of another independence referendum, the launch and resetting of a referendum campaign and the delaying and blocking devices of the UK government through the medium of the 2017 UK general election. It's hard to know where we are in all of this given the political events of the last year.

Whilst public opinion hasn't really changed on independence as we shall see – there was a sense in which the clock was ticking on #ScotRef in the months following the Brexit vote. For example, the Scottish Government published a second draft independence referendum bill at the end of 2016 and, significantly, undertook a large consultation on independence through the National Survey that finished on 30th November 2016 (with over 2 million respondents). This survey occurred before the appearance of a hard Brexit prospectus by the UK government (which appeared to soften post-June 2017), but if it generated a lot of useful data on the independence issue, it might provide both strategic political guidance and also practical ground campaign support for the battle to come (so we're not starting from scratch with voter data like we did in 2012). The SNP also established a Growth Commission to help rework the economics of independence in advance of any new independence referendum and the Scottish Government has also undertaken significant work on Scotland's role in the post-Brexit European Union to protect Scotland's economic and social interests (including some lobbying of the EU and member states). So, it certainly hasn't been all quiet on the referendum front – but rather a period of gathering background work and preparation to lay the ground for a second referendum. When you understand it in those terms, you realise that Nicola Sturgeon's 'shock' announcement about a second independence referendum wasn't actually such a shock at all. We still aren't clear when the new referendum will occur – and under what rules and regulations – and we don't know its economic and political circumstances. But, the redubbed ScotRef appeared

Alison Johnstone MSP speaks at Scotland to Remain demonstration at Scottish Parliament in Holyrood 29ᵗʰ June 2016.

on the starting blocks with the SNP launching its campaign on Monday 13th March 2017.

Of course, immediately, this launch brought two responses. Scotland in Union launched a campaign against a referendum on the 14th March (please remember that they are active, have staff and are successfully raising funds – don't underestimate your opponents), Theresa May then blocked the process by saying "now is not the time" on Thursday 16th March and then the referendum issue was a feature of the local election campaign enthusiastically adopted by the Conservatives as a one-slogan mantra. Now, quite clearly, the Conservative message was both clear and unclear – "now is not the time" and "no means no" are totally different messages and would appeal to slightly different voters. However, they certainly helped to get Conservative voters to turn out at the election and to see the party also gain voters through its hard Unionist message. Then the UK general election was called and the anti-referendum message, plus clever repositioning on Brexit, helped the Tories to their best result in Scotland since 1992 – at the expense of the SNP. And this latter event had a sobering effect on the SNP and the prospects of ScotRef: and that's something Yessers need to come to terms with. Politics shifted at the general election and the implications of that need to be digested not ignored.

Yes Is Still Going

One of the funny things about the referendum of 2014 is how much Yes has continued long after the event itself: evidence that the issue and long campaign did give birth to a functioning Yes movement (even if the internal shenanigans of summer 2017 indicated it wasn't such a mature political movement). A lot of Yessers have gone into the SNP, a fair number into the Scottish Greens and many of these activists have been diverted into election campaigning since the 2014 referendum. Others have found expression in a range of organisations and initiatives, though how permanent or fragile these new organisations are remains to be seen. Some on the left continued to run Radical Independence, which worked away on the Scottish Left Project to create a new leftist party in Scotland: officially launched as RISE on 29th August 2015. However its performance at the Scottish election of 2016 was nothing short of disastrous. RIC's national and local groups continued to campaign

The EU referendum count at Meadowbank Stadium, Edinburgh, 23rd June 2016.

after the election though, with its national conference, local meetings and campaigning against the arms trade, racism, etc. But, its role and impact has its limits now just as it did at the referendum. Women for Independence meantime, is bigger than ever. It has institutionalised, decentralised to go local, and picked a range of campaigns to become active on: opposition to the women's super prison in Greenock, violence against women, women in the media, women's experiences in the justice system etc.[18] Business for Scotland has continued to operate and has been running a confidence-building crowd-funded social media campaign on Scotland's economy. Phantom Power's *Journey to Yes* film series has also been a prominent online presence, spreading the No-to-Yes message featuring voters who have changed their mind. Local groups have remained active, some organized into the National Yes Registry,[19] with local meetings, shops and cafes still operational. There isn't a unified national Yes campaign as such – yet there remains a capacity to fall out via Twitter – though there is continued networking and discussion such as the Scottish Independence Convention conference in Glasgow in January 2017. Groups like Common Weal have emerged more fully, with its local groups, publications, policy work on independence, the Common Space news service and Common Market online shopping network, alongside other independent media sources as well as the new pro-independence daily newspaper, *The National*. The semblance of a Yes media has been established as a sustainable alternative to the mainstream media for the time being – though it remains much smaller and weakly funded. Finally, look around you and you'll still see people with Yes badges, Yes stickers on cars and even posters in windows. See a white van go past and some still retain a wee, blue Yes Scotland sticker on it. Some people de-Yessed after the referendum, but a lot continued to project the issue and the Yes concept. Despite everything that's happened since 2014, there's still an active yet imperfect Yes movement out there, with its groups, meetings, social media and occasional rallies. The problem might be that it can spend its time talking to itself – either in person or through social media – so it has become a self-reinforcing echo chamber, rather than a movement that connects with the public in the way it did from 2012-14. And, you can bet some of this has continued into 2017, helping to reinforce rather than span the Yes-No political divide when there still aren't enough Yes voters to win the referendum.

Coming Soon – ScotRef?

We've all probably still got the old t-shirts for the next referendum, but that doesn't mean we should rush into it – even with the Brexit trigger. Are we ready for the next one? Not exactly. And that's a problem as campaigning time is short, even when it seems like it is abundant. If ScotRef were to happen in the autumn of 2018 before the actual Brexit date on March 2019, it would be the third referendum in four years (to accompany five sets of elections). Think how that would be received by voters – not by us, the political geeks or the *Spinal Tap* Yessers – but by ordinary people. Not with enthusiasm I'd bet. There's been a lot of politics of late and not everyone would welcome more in the short-term. The 'extra' election in 2017 didn't help for sure.

And, in some senses, the fact we've had several referendums presents a quite illusory picture. Though it might seem that the referendum device has become a normal feature of politics in Scotland and the UK, that's far from accurate. There have only been three UK-wide referendums. Scotland has had only one 'official' referendum since devolution was established in 1999 and it was on independence: that means no referendum on Calman or Smith, none on same-sex marriage or minimum alcohol pricing or the smoking ban. Edinburgh and Aberdeen councils held local referendums and Brian Soutar financed his own on the teaching of homosexuality in schools, but it's not as if we can claim referendums are a popular device in Scotland. It might seem like referendums are in more frequent use here but we're very far from being Switzerland or some of the US states that hold referendums through local initiatives most years.

Also, remember the long 18 years between the first Scottish and Welsh devolution referendums of 1979 and the second ones in 1997. A second independence referendum may seem inevitable, but it might not follow on so quickly from the first one in 2014. We could be waiting a long time time for ScotRef, despite Brexit and notions of momentum and material changes. The Yes side wants one before Brexit occurs, the UK Government doesn't want one at all and will argue for a longer timescale in any case – to ensure Scotland leaves the EU before ScotRef and disenfranchise EU citizens, thus making a Yes vote notionally harder (and they were negotiating this in public in the days followed the March announcement just like last time), then used the council and general elections of 2017 to campaign unequivocally against another independence referendum. Third, the fact that Yes started on approximately 25 per cent at the Scottish election in May 2011[20] and ended up on 45 per cent in 2014 does not mean that Yes campaigners can simply 'bank' the 45 per cent and accumulate additional votes: political life isn't that simple. The political and economic conditions of 2014 will not be those of the ScotRef and voters may well have changed their minds in both directions – with a churn in voters between Yes, No and undecided. I'm not suggesting Yes (and No) will be starting from scratch at any future independence referendum, but do not assume Yes is starting from a high level. Similarly, do not assume that undecideds will all plump for Yes next time around or that Yes cannot lose supporters to the other side either. These were unpredictable before Brexit threw up the prospect of people moving from Yes to No in order to back up their support for exiting the EU – potentially cancelling out the movement from No to Yes on the same issue.

The EU issue – and alternatives like the EEA and EFTA – are complicating factors right now in the independence debate and certainly next time around at a referendum too. There is likely to be some considerable repositioning by all sides on Europe before another independence referendum. Brexit may have triggered ScotRef in principle but it has also partly fractured both the Yes and No voter base from 2014. The EU was not an unimportant issue last time – both Yes and No built their cases for independence and the Union in 2014 on the basis of EU membership. Brexit changed all that – not least as Scotland voted to Remain by 62 per cent, whilst England voted to Leave by 53.4 per cent (the UK result was 51.9 per cent Leave to 48.1 per cent Remain). Brexit changes everything about the constitutional issue and the politics and economics of Scotland though voters may not have registered this in the way we'd like. Brexit also doesn't make independence inevitable. Not least as many Scottish independence voters supported Brexit. When the SNP adjusted its independence goal in the 1980s to one of Independence in Europe, it did so because it wanted Scotland to be part of a European single market umbrella that would guarantee Scottish access to the UK and EU markets: the EU was an external support system for Scotland in the UK, as well as for the growing EU. Independence in Europe was adopted in an EU of 12. Now, we have an EU of 28 (including the UK for now). Brexit therefore challenges the policy of Independence in Europe – hence the Scottish Government focus on single market access, a soft UK Brexit and discussion of alternatives like the EEA and EFTA.[21] Independence is not any less complicated with Brexit and some of the arguments from 2014 have already resurfaced in familiar ways – about hard borders for example and the importance of the UK single market to Scotland. Of course, Brexit and a potential hard Brexit also undermine some of Better Together's arguments from 2014 – can they now accuse anyone of division? – and the economic realities of a Conservative government make notions of 'pooling and sharing' rather comical (unless you are the DUP in Northern Ireland of course). Both Yes and No will need some different positions and arguments next time around as some are now redundant. However, overall, there's no escaping the likely economic and political damage of Brexit, which will be felt across the public and private sectors in Scotland so there is a strong impetus to escape this damage through a second independence referendum before the UK actually exits the European Union. However, unless something totally unexpected happens Brexit will happen and I'm not sure voters grasp the reality of Brexit and its effects either.

Are Good The Politics Good?

Is the political environment conducive to success for Yes at a second independence referendum? Before Brexit, the idea of a second independence referendum suffered from the proximity of the 2014 experience and result. Something big would have needed to occur to legitimise the argument for ScotRef – even then, some time might have to pass to ensure success next time around. Otherwise, the issue could be kicked into the long grass for a period until something turned up – leading us all to think of the next referendum after the planned UK general election of 2020 (which actually occurred in June 2017) or the Scottish election of 2021 (or much, much longer). However, political life can produce surprises like Brexit to hurry things along or the 2017 general election to slow them down. After 2014, 'next time' was a political dilemma for the SNP that it had to manage. The referendum had seen its membership and its support grow – and it had to balance this support with the need to win votes from new and non-independence supporters through the 2015 and 2016 elections and avoid losing potential support from appearing obsessed with independence when it had lost the referendum. It also had to balance the views of a grassroots that was divided on the speed of the next referendum. The route out of this dilemma came, in 2016, through the party's Scottish election manifesto. Here the party's referendum position was that:

> We believe that the Scottish Parliament should have the right to hold another referendum if there is clear and sustained evidence that independence has become the preferred option of a majority of the Scottish people – or if there is a significant and material change in the circumstances that prevailed in 2014, such as Scotland being taken out of the EU against our will.[22]

This particular formula helped the SNP progress through the Scottish election – as by far the largest party – although it failed to retain its overall parliamentary majority. As we shall see, the policy was to provide a considerable trigger for a second referendum – with a significant and material change of circumstances – but not clear and sustained evidence of majority support for independence: far from it.

The politics are complicated however and fall into two phases. In 2016, the politics looked positive because of the political strength of the SNP and then the Brexit trigger itself – which assumed that Brexit would transform the voter landscape on independence. At the 2016 Scottish election, the SNP vote went up to 46.5 per cent in the constituency vote, with 1,059,897 votes, even though its list vote dipped and it lost its majority. Its constituency vote total was more than that of the Conservatives and Labour combined, and Labour fell back to third place. At the same time as the SNP had come to dominate political representation, the main No party in Scotland, Labour, collapsed. Members, resources and electoral representation shifted decisively in the SNP's favour in 2011, 2015 and 2016 and Labour's political infrastructure in Scotland shrunk: meaning all those MPs, their staff, media presence etc. A Labour-led No campaign in Scotland looked unlikely in the future. Labour also looked unelectable in Scotland and at the UK level in 2015 and 2016. The Scottish election gave the SNP 63 out of 129 MSPs (down from 69 in 2011) to make it a large minority government in a parliament with an independence majority, when you add the six Green MSPs (compare the SNP's minority status now to that of 2007-11 and realise it's a world away). However, the result gave the SNP a clear political mandate to govern and arguably a mandate to ask to hold another referendum – combining with the Green MSPs – and, with the legitimacy of a material change in circumstances signaled in the 2016 manifesto, came the 2017 ScotRef announcement. Political conditions at Westminster seemed positive too – a majority Conservative government until 2020 and, given the state of Labour at the time, perhaps until 2025.

And then it all changed with the snap general election of June 2017 – and especially in the last couple of weeks of the campaign. Gerry Hassan's idea of 'peak SNP' has some traction as the party fell dramatically at the UK general election as all parties took seats and votes from the SNP. Tactical voting by anti-independence and anti-SNP supporters had developed at the 2016 Scottish election and was evident at the council elections too. The ScotRef announcement occurred during the council campaign and before the general election announcement – and it made sure the independence referendum was a big issue at the general election which reinforced some of the messages of the anti-independence parties. The electorate were voting on other things too, so over-determining the result as being solely about independence isn't accurate.[23] However, after the 2017 election the political environment prevalent in 2016 no longer applies – we now have a shaky Conservative Government, a shrunken

SNP contingent at Westminster coming to terms with a huge loss of support (and it could have been worse), electoral recovery in Scotland from the Conservatives, Labour and Liberal Democrats. Significantly, Labour at the UK level is now definitely electable and has a popular leader too.

Opinion Polls and Independence

Whilst at one level, the politics look less positive in late 2017 than they did earlier in the same year, one clear additional problem is that the electorate doesn't seem to have changed its mind that much on independence, even with Brexit. A referendum data study by Common Weal in January 2017 found that little had changed compared to 2014, though there were some marginal changes in support for Yes and No (Dalzell 2017). In recent years, some polls have given Yes a narrow lead over No – YouGov had it at 52 per cent to 48 per cent when undecideds were excluded in November 2014 and February 2015.[24] Ipsos-MORI had Yes ahead by 53 per cent to 44 per cent, with 3 per cent undecided in September 2015.[25] TNS put Yes at 47 per cent, No at 42 per cent and don't knows at 15 per cent in September 2015 (53 per cent to 47 per cent when don't knows were excluded).[26] However Survation had No leading by 46.6 per cent to 43.3 per cent on 8th July 2015 and Panelbase had No ahead by 50 per cent to 45 per cent on 21st July 2015. Even the opinion poll that gave the SNP 62 per cent support for the constituency vote at the 2016 Holyrood election,[27] came on the back of opinion polls that put Yes at 43 per cent and No at 47 per cent in July 2015:[28] and that 62 per cent was hugely optimistic too as it turned out. Into 2016, there were no real changes in the pattern of support for independence in opinion polls that would guarantee a different outcome from 2014. The highest Yes vote was 49 per cent in February and the lowest Yes vote was 40 per cent in March 2016. The highest No vote was 51 per cent in February and April 2016. And, in May 2016, the polls showed 41 per cent for Yes, 48 per cent for No and 12 per cent as undecided.[29] There were also six different opinion polls sampling the effect of Brexit on Scottish independence from January to April 2016 – asking 'if the UK leaves the EU, how would you vote at a future Scottish independence referendum?' Sure enough, Brexit did change opinion slightly but not dramatically. The highest Yes vote was 54 per cent in February 2016 to

39 per cent No. The last poll in April, saw Yes on 47 per cent, No on 44 per cent, with 9 per cent undecided:[30] so, nothing decisive in the short–term before the June 2016 referendum either.

However, at this stage, the Brexit referendum arrived to change the political and economic environment of Scottish constitutional politics. After Brexit, Yes saw leads of 47 to 41 per cent in June 2016 but this slid throughout the year to sit at 40 per cent for Yes and 47 per cent No, with 9 per cent undecided in December 2016.[31] It's not as if Yes has collapsed, rather that both the Yes and No options fluctuate within certain levels. However, in no way could it be argued that a clear and sustained majority for Yes exists, even with the material change of Brexit – so far at any rate. And, into 2017, the first opinion polls on independence found the clock stuck at 10pm on 18th September 2014: with 45.5 per cent Yes to 54.5 per cent No, though 61.5 per cent were opposed to a second independence referendum during 2017 too.[32] The 50-50 per cent poll for STV on 4th March 2017[33] gave Yes supporters hope before the First Minister's ScotRef announcement but it doesn't actually indicate that much change – compare it to the pre-2014 opinion polls that gave No some huge leads over Yes and you realise that although its position might seem to be strengthening, Yes has trouble breeching the 50% barrier. The last polls before the UK general election on 7th June had Yes at 41 or 36 per cent, No at 53 or 56 per cent and 7 or 6 per cent undecided (with the remaining small % refusing to answer).[34]

So, in short, whilst we have a huge material change and a huge event in Brexit, that disrupts the political, economic and constitutional environment, this is yet to disturb previous voter behaviour on independence even when Brexit was factored into independence opinion poll questions. Of course, with the Brexit issue as with anything else, public opinion can change with time. It can take some time for the altered political and economic conditions to sink in with voters: remember how there was only a slight majority in support of devolution in 1979, but it had become a landslide by 1997? However, there isn't really that much cheer to be taken from the polls <u>at present</u> – and I stress <u>at present</u>, as support may change. The big plus is that Yes seems to have solidified. However, support for No remains large and often larger. It's not as if Yes is now sitting on 65 per cent support. It's still very marginal when in the lead in opinion polls and sometimes within the margin of error, even with the material change of Brexit (and that's before getting to the issue of differential turnout, with No voters being more likely to vote than Yes voters).[35] Something we saw all too well in Edinburgh Western in 2014, despite our efforts to counteract it through extensive voter registration and mobilisation efforts.

What About Those Economics?

When you look at the economic environment, not much has changed to assist the case for independence besides Brexit (which is huge of course). Sure enough, continued Conservative austerity has an impact but key things like the oil price (despite its recent rise) and its effect on Scottish employment have gone in the wrong direction. The Scottish Government is set to receive some devolved powers to help shape economic development, but there needs to be a demonstrable change in Scotland's economic performance that convinces voters, businesses and some key organisations that Scotland can survive and thrive (or that Brexit is so economically damaging, independence is vital). The fact that parts of the Scottish economy are integrated into the wider UK economy is a problematic fact of life. It was one of the main reasons the SNP argued for currency union, through the medium of the Fiscal Commission of economic experts. Whatever you might think about the idea of currency union, it didn't deliver a Yes vote though. The other currency alternatives would probably not have fared any better mind you – each would have been attacked by Better Together, the UK Government and London-based political parties. And they will be next time too, heavily. If you think a Scottish currency is going to be the magic bullet at ScotRef, you need to think about what the No campaign will say and what voters will think. Enjoy explaining that on the doorsteps when the time comes.

Moreover, despite Scotland having a pretty strong economy, I'm not sure voters believe it. We can be a pessimistic lot at the best of times, but the economic background to the 2014 referendum was not an encouraging one. We would have faced an uphill battle in any event, but the Great Financial Crisis of 2008 created substantial and real problems for Scottish independence – about finance, currency, tax and spending, banking and a host of other issues like the EU bailouts of Greece, Portugal, Ireland and Spain. None of these real events helped the cause of Scottish independence. We were trying to launch a new state into stormy weather and strong economic headwinds. Voters had seen the boom and were now experiencing the bust and all that meant for incomes, cost of living, job prospects, savings, pensions and employment. It was hard to argue with the caution of some people in Edinburgh Western who worked in the finance industry as RBS and HBOS shrank through redundancies despite the taxpayer bailouts. The Great Financial Crisis opened up political debate for some within the electorate – which the anti-austerity Yes campaign sought to exploit – but it created problems and made 'risk' a reality for a lot of other voters as the referendum occurred in some of the hardest of hard economic times. It made some of the 'wicked issues'[36] even more wicked to deal with in the campaign at every level – TV studio and doorstep (Maxwell 2012). Even so, money isn't everything. I remember making an economic pitch about independence to a female voter in Clerwood in Edinburgh Western only to get blank looks as she explained she didn't care about money and would base her vote on quality of life issues and whether we would have a better society in the future: an ideal candidate for a Green Yes appeal. If we'd had more of those voters, things might have turned out differently. However, the politics and economics of risk and uncertainty were strong in 2014 and a successful part of Better Together's pitch to undecided voters at the referendum: it will likely prove so again in a future independence referendum and has already started.

'Don't wait until the campaign starts before starting to campaign', says Common Weal's Robin McAlpine.

16
Getting It Right Next Time

Let's put all the qualifications from the previous chapter to one side and imagine there will be a second Scottish independence referendum in the near-ish future. That prospect would raise three questions in my mind – as well as feelings of mild panic. First, when exactly would it be? I am not a fan of indulging in the game of fantasy referendum dates but timing is important as the date acts as a trigger for campaigners. How can we campaign for something when we don't know exactly what it is, when it is or whether we'll be able to do it? Those are all problems. But building support for independence and addressing some of its perceived shortcomings does not need an actual referendum date. The current state of politics means we also need to be patient. Patience does not mean inertia though. There's enough of a grassroots in existence plus a series of organisations with campaign capacity to make some progress, without having to rely solely on a Scottish Government that is busy with the difficult task of governing. Second, what would be the case for Yes next time? Third, what do we – the folk on the ground – do between now and then and at the campaign itself? (and I know there is some activist burnout there too – so asking campaigners to go to the well one more time is tricky).

Timing is difficult because of political and economic factors as well as process issues – about mandates, timetables, section 30 orders, etc. Whilst the right to hold a referendum is heavily contested in a much more polarised environment than last time, timing will be shaped by either the Brexit timetable now that Article 50 has been triggered (with the UK departing the EU in April 2019) or something like the result and mandate of a future UK general election or the Scottish election of 2021. This is exactly what was being argued between the Scottish and UK governments in early 2017 before the UK general election of 8th

June intervened to throw confusion over the notion of a timetable at all. UK politics is in flux at present and it's difficult to know what this means for the independence question – all we have is speculation. Will the current Conservative minority government survive? Will there be a new election or just a new PM? Will Labour's recovery see it win power at Westminster in another snap general election or the next scheduled UK election in 2022? How will the voters assess the independence issue at the Scottish election in 2021? What form will Brexit take? We don't know. Peering into the future with any degree of certainty here is brain-scrambling and any referendum timetable may not suit the case for Yes at all.

The point about the timetable is to be realistic about what it means for the campaign – not make heroic assumptions about what Yes or the SNP can deliver during a campaign when politics can spring surprises. Elections and referendums are not processions – as Theresa May discovered on 8th June. Even within the short 2017 campaign, the received wisdom of a Conservative landslide evaporated as Labour recovered and grew its support, despite predictions it would do worse than in 2015. May started the election popular and ended up unpopular – even though electoral support for her party rose. Jeremy Corbyn experienced a complete reversal in public opinion about his leadership and, post-election, Labour led UK opinion polls to transform the unelectable into the very electable. The point here is we have unpredictability and change in a time of turbulent politics – and surprise events like the general election disturbed preparations and assumptions about ScotRef.

Imagine if Brexit determined the date so that we were looking at ScotRef sometime between Autumn 2018 and Spring 2019. This timing would place a significant constraint on what any of us could hope to do in relation to campaigning. It may seem like there is ample campaign time, but that time will disappear quickly. A later referendum date linked to election mandates might create a longer timescale for campaign planning and delivery. But that's assuming that ScotRef is like Indyref – negotiated between the two governments and delivered with a section 30 order. However, the current UK government not only opposes a second independence referendum but built its Scottish electoral recovery on completely ruling out a second referendum: there's a huge u-turn to think about there before even getting to the fragile nature of the Conservative's minority government and the role of the DUP on the issue.

UK government agreement for a second independence referendum is therefore unlikely at this stage. Don't rule out the Scottish Government holding its own advisory referendum and perhaps asking something about the EEA not the EU as part of the question either though – it needs to be tactically nimble here about what it can do. However, we're in very uncertain times here on the constitutional question and the nature of Brexit and how they will play out.

In relation to the exact nature of the Yes prospectus next time around, well, there is likely to be argument and contestation and, with an early referendum, not much time to develop new positions and campaign on them. It's not hard to see how the content of the Yes offer next time around is likely to be a contested one amongst the Yes movement. In 2014, there was an official set of proposals for independence from the Scottish Government in the shape of the White Paper *Scotland's Future*, as well as less detailed Green and radical versions of independence. These differed on the currency, NATO membership and monarchy and presented a broader set of themes – and conflicts – for Yes than just the White Paper. For ScotRef, we may see a repeat of this, with official SNP and Scottish Government plans influenced by the Growth Commission report and EU context and alternatives, whilst other options are laid on the table on issues like currency by the Greens and the Common Weal's White Paper project (Common Weal 2017). And, presenting a Yes prospectus in light of Brexit is a challenge – though one the Scottish Government has worked on several times from 2012-14 and currently. The issue of Brexit is likely to dominate Scottish and UK politics for the next few years and beyond that too. The reason for this is simply that it is a vast, multi-dimensional issue. It is a constitutional issue directly connected to the politics of Scottish independence but it also has so many practical policy aspects to it too, that connect to the economy, business, trade unions, environmental groups, higher education, food standards, science and just about everything else. We joined the European Union in 1973 and this means there are over 40 years of common policy to disentangle, not least in areas like agriculture and fisheries where Scottish and UK policy equals European policy. It's hard to get across how large and all-encompassing this is. The work programmes of Scottish and UK civil servants and Ministers will be dominated by the huge agenda involved up to and beyond the Brexit date itself.

However, whatever the Yes prospectus is next time around, getting it across to voters on the doorsteps of Drum Brae or Muirhouse is what most of us will be involved with: not designing the prospectus itself. Unless there is huge support for Yes and the task becomes one of turning out supporters rather than converting undecided or No voters – which is my memory of the 1997 devolution referendum – then we are in for a real challenge, especially if the referendum falls in the next couple of years. We may not see a repeat of the 28 month referendum campaign that led up to 2014, an experience which allowed a grassroots campaign to grow and develop, though some of this has survived in any case and is still running. Then again, if the UK government sticks to its blocking position, maybe we will.

So, whilst campaign time may be shorter next time, there is still the need for grassroots activity across Scotland. So, what did we learn from 2014 and what could be done better next time? It's not as if we are drowning in local or national post-mortems after 2014 so it's unclear what we have learned from the experience and need to relearn or unlearn. Have we actually looked back and thought through what worked and figured out what we would change next time? And, remember, ScotRef will be both similar and different compared to the first time around. It will have a slightly different electorate, as some voters will have died, some young voters will enter the electorate each year as they reach 16 years old and there will be new people who come to live in Scotland from other parts of the UK and around the world. So, it's not the same as in 2014 and lots of things will have changed, not least as campaigning has moved online via Google Analytics, Facebook advertising, dark advertising and covert funding (as the DUP's actions during the Brexit referendum illustrated).[37] However, here are some things to think about. And the point is to think and also to plan. Like last time, a lot of our job is to engage people and discuss the issues with them, using traditional and imaginative political campaigning. I'm pretty sure a fair section of the electorate is not enthusiastic for any full-on referendum campaigning at the minute but there are plenty of things to reflect upon and some opportunities for campaigners too – and only you know what's deliverable on the ground in your area and what isn't.

1. Have You Started Yet?

A good starting point is a very simple one – what are you doing now? If you are in a political party, is that party actually collecting data on independence or is that something to be left until the campaign itself? If the latter is the answer, then you're in trouble. As Robin McAlpine pointed out, don't wait until the campaign starts to do some campaigning (2016: 13). A last minute effort is unlikely to succeed, especially if it's a short campaign. It's not just whether you know who the Yes, No and undecided are but what kind they are too? Are they Labour undecideds, SNP No voters, or voters completely undecided on party preference and the constitutional question? Are they male or female, old or young, etc? Were they Yes-Leave, Yes-Remain, No-Remain or No-Leave? – additional complications for the campaign to come as Brexit has moved Yes and No voters around (and moved voters around at the 2017 general election too). There are a lot of questions here about demographics and local knowledge to consider. Leaving it until the campaign itself, whenever it comes, won't help. If it's a short campaign, it will be even harder. And, no one is going to do this for you. If you are a SNP supporter hoping that the National Survey will do the work for you, ask yourself what you'd do if you had the survey data yourself? What would you do with it and when? Have you been promoting the SNP's 'mobilise' online site (http://www.mobilise.scot/) – something not dissimilar to the National Survey and the Yes Declaration in its potential to help generate an active grassroots for independence. Similarly, if you are a local Yes group, do you have a draft ground campaign ready, are campaigners trained and ready, do you have fundraising in place or a business plan? Or are we all going to stumble into the ScotRef as under prepared as we were in 2014 and just hope for the best?

2. The Infrastructure of Yes

In 2014, it took a long time for the infrastructure of Yes to get up and running. It did end up with hundreds of active groups though and thousands of members of which many are still active and have graduated into slightly new roles and functions. The question is whether you are participating in them or funding of them? Because we've had so many elections of late, many political activists were diverted naturally enough into party-based campaigning. However, we are not short of Yes groups on the ground – hence the National Yes Registry tour of Scotland in the summer of 2017 or *The National*'s promotional tour of Scotland, talks by Paul Kavanagh or the many local Common Weal groups. In spite of ScotRef being a principle backed by legislative mandate rather than a concrete reality, we have a nascent Yes campaign still functioning and lots going on. So, if you're wondering what to do or concerned that no one is doing anything about the referendum – you're not only wrong but there are lots of opportunities to get involved. So, get the proverbial finger out. It's not as if we're short of campaign groups to crowdfund or support.

3. Hard Work

Ground campaigning is hard work and you need to start it some time and stick at it. It needs to be systematic not sporadic and it takes time, people and money on the ground (and light and sunshine). It can be a slow grind at times with periods of panic and worry at other times. For us, the hard work was in keeping it going over a long period of time – we started when we didn't actually know the date of the referendum itself – and then maintaining it as new people joined the campaign. This last part was difficult. Sometimes, we were small in numbers – only 2-3 going out canvassing – and had to keep ourselves going: a joyous festival of democracy this was not. At other times, new activists came in waves – after the 2012 and 2013 independence marches, at the turn of the year into 2014 and then across the summer. As the referendum approached there was a bit of a bandwagon effect as people wanted to get involved – though, too many came late to the party. Last minute enthusiasm wasn't actually much use – there was no time to train new canvassers as we were all too busy campaigning. Dealing with latecomers also distracted from organising things like the Get Out The Vote. However, the plus side of all the work was that we were methodical, canvassing was professional, data was logged and used where we could (revisiting undecideds and ensuring they had the Yes conversion booklet), we used the database to aid voter registration and the GOTV at the end, focused on four key parts of Edinburgh Western. We needed the Yes Scotland organisation for this mind you. It's hard to do this as an autonomous Yes group in the absence of an actual referendum. Hence point 4 immediately below.

4. Voter Registration

For quite a large part of the campaign, leading up to the last day of voter registration, we went in search of the 'missing million'. We were determined and meticulous, using the electoral register, the Yes database and local knowledge to embark on a sustained voter registration campaign. We had forms, envelopes, information on voting and some of us spent time explaining the what, where, when and how of voting to people who had fallen off the register or who'd never been on it in the first place: the referendum would be the first time they would vote. We had to explain the difference between the public and private registers and also the likelihood of people being 'found' by debt collectors if they registered to vote. We did all this under the old registration process, in which whole households would be registered. Since 2014, electoral registration occurs through individual registration and can be achieved online but requires some personal identification such as a national insurance number, which makes registration is a little trickier. The new process plus the general churn of voters through the housing market has meant that voters have moved off of the register. So, in addition to seeing voting experience a decreased turnout since the high point of 2014, registrations have declined. Thus, to some extent we're starting all over again. The point here is – let's not go through all that again. If you're in a party, do registration now – don't leave it until the campaign to go in search of the 'missing million'. If you have a Yes group, get it out registering rather than talking to itself in meetings. And, whilst the old registration process was simple – you were either registered or you weren't – now it's more unpredictable as voters register via monthly updates, can do so online or transfer their registration from an old address or local authority. It's a lot less black and white to know who's on or off the electoral register now.

5. Talking and Listening

Talking and listening were key aspects of what we did in 2014. We doorstepped all sorts of voters and did so systematically – but not all the voters by any means as we didn't have the people. We also sought to discuss the independence issue with them and I mean <u>discuss</u>: conversation was key. We canvassed sympathetic areas, some unsympathetic areas and also held 70 plus information stalls. We held public meetings and generally sought as many opportunities as we could to talk <u>with</u> the public – not talk <u>at</u> the public. Occasionally we had canvassers who wanted to lecture voters on their own doorsteps, which is rarely a good idea and often unproductive. Our best canvassers were gentle persuaders who used their own experiences to talk about independence and help people relate to it. And, because of the limited conversion efforts by Yes Scotland, we ended up revisiting our undecided voters on their doorsteps too. Again, conversations were key, as well as delivering the Yes booklet for undecideds that was intended to reach a range of different types of voter (I usually pointed voters to the Bob Holman feature inside). We fielded as many questions as we could – and the referendum involved every topic under the sun. In campaigning terms, this was old hat and very traditional campaign activity. But, it gave us an opportunity to talk with people in order to gauge their reactions, opinions, feelings and reflections and also talk about various aspects of politics with them – explain independence, devolution, devolved powers, the economy, etc. – all things you'd struggle to do on social media. You won't win independence via Twitter, not least because your grandparents aren't on it. You need to be talking with people and listening to what they say – especially women voters.[38] You can't just try to thump people over the head with facts and arguments like a debating society – though, to be absolutely clear, voters do need facts: it's what they are and how you deliver them that is important.

6. Structural/Demographic Factors

Anyone who didn't notice the different socio-economic composition of the Yes-No vote wasn't paying attention. There was strong working class support for Yes in many areas and more middle class support for No in others. You could actually go area to area and predict the likelihood of referendum vote by housing type – not as a 100 per cent rule but as a probability. No voters were wealthier, owned their houses, tended to have landlines and postal votes and also, significantly, were habitual voters. The fact they were longer-term residents in their homes – with postal votes – helped them to vote. A total of 796,835 postal votes were cast in 2014 – 18.6 per cent of the total. They contrasted markedly with the people we met who were part of Edinburgh's large rental sector, moving home on several occasions and not having landlines or postal votes. They were the people we had to register and try to turn into habitual voters. It wasn't easy. In fact, it put us at a permanent disadvantage, as we had to spend time registering them rather than converting others. However, there was no point having all these potential – and actual – Yes supporters unregistered and unable to vote on 18th September. That really was a losing campaign strategy. However, it's important not to learn the wrong lesson here – meaning, let's abandon working class areas of low turnout and all head down to the middle class suburbs to win independence (yes, people have actually suggested this). A more fruitful strategy is to aim to increase independence support in working class communities whilst campaigning amongst middle class voters too.

7. Yes Scotland Database and the 1-10 Scale

The Yes Scotland database in 2014 was completely inadequate and not well-used. It did some basic things well, in terms of logging support and identifying Yes/No/undecided and helping to target some campaigning, but that's all it did. It helped with voter registration for a while but wasn't much use for targeting. It only asked two questions – asking people about their constitutional preference on a 1-10 scale (if 1 is completely in favour of the Union and 10 is completely in favour of independence) and whether they were Yes, No or undecided. But that was it. So, we didn't know whether the person was a Labour No, a Lib Dem Yes or a Conservative undecided. We didn't know whether they were Green or SNP or anything else and we didn't know anything about their demographics. Very late in the campaign, Yes Scotland did send us target demographic canvass lists to work on, though these were a bit hit and miss in terms of results (we did do them though and found Yes supporters). So, there is a challenge for the Yes parties here in recording and utilising data much more effectively than last time around.

8. SNP Supporters Who Are No

As mentioned above in relation to data collection, there are SNP supporters who are No and undecided on independence. This fact might surprise you but some people are absolute 100 per cent SNP voters but worry about independence. Better Together canvassers saw this quite clearly at the referendum and so did Yes campaigners when they delved into party preferences on the doorsteps. This is a problem the SNP has to think about and, I'd imagine the Greens do too – how to convince their own supporters to support independence. This is a serious issue to tackle as it might involve voters in the hundreds of thousands. Leaving it until the ScotRef campaign is underway is not advisable either (and yet here we are!).

9. Yes But Not Now

Another group of voters to think about were the 'Yes but not now' brigade. They were a special category of undecideds, people who quite liked the idea of independence and were warm towards it, but worried about timing: often meaning they were worried about Scotland becoming independent in a poor economic climate or wanted a stronger devolved Scotland before they felt secure enough to vote Yes. There's certainly a case for more institution-building and nation-building in Scotland to help reduce the gap between wanting to vote Yes and actually doing so, but there's not an awful lot of time to address this if we're looking at an early referendum.

10. Do It Yourself

Finally, don't look to Yes Scotland or a political party to solve your problems on the ground at ScotRef. Local politicians might not be of much help either. Whether the next independence referendum campaign is long or short, to a certain extent, the local campaigners have to run the campaign and troubleshoot all the problems that can emerge. You need to get on with it and stop looking for an organisational hierarchy to solve campaign problems – though I realise how frustrating this can be during a campaign. But, if you have a Yes group, ask yourself this – what is the skill base of local members? Are there graphic designers or database geeks or people who can organise target letters? Have local supporters been trained or socialised into becoming activists or will we all just hope this will kick in during a campaign? And, try to think about making campaigns more imaginative to engage people. We certainly got the basics right in terms of public meetings, canvassing, stalls and leafleting – and the pre-referendum festival in Drylaw and Muirhouse. We were reasonably effective at these but beyond these, we were reliant on Yes Scotland or other organisations to produce materials, run social media, publicity, etc., and that was a problem throughout.

Let's get back out there. If we don't, who else will?

References

1. In Edinburgh, the number 14 bus travels between Muirhouse and Craigmillar: two working class housing schemes that were prominent Yes areas in 2014.
2. And, if you wonder why I've named so few fellow campaigners in this book, when there were so many in my local area – that's the reason why.
3. See https://www.flickr.com/photos/scottishpoliticalarchive/
4. These were 4 prominent Labour politicians – Roy Jenkins, David Owen, Bill Rodgers ands Shirley Williams.
5. All figures taken from House of Commons library's constituency explorer area profile for Edinburgh West, using the 2011 census information. See www.constituencyexplorer.org.uk
6. Scottish Neighbourhood Statistics Report, *Area Profile report for 2011 Scottish Parliamentary Constituency Edinburgh Western*.
7. http://www.edinburghnews.scotsman.com/news/crime/syrian-doctor-had-bomb-materials-in-leith-flat-1-3702702
8. For her poetry/cabaret work see http://rallyandbroad.com and https://flintandpitch.com
9. You can watch the encounter here on the BBC – http://news.bbc.co.uk/1/hi/8649853.stm
10. http://www.edinburghnews.scotsman.com/news/edinburgh-has-highest-rate-of-migrants-in-scotland-1-3218339
11. http://news.stv.tv/scotland/295133-scotland-tonight-documentary-charts-spanish-immigration-to-capital/
12. Figures taken from House of Commons library's constituency explorer area profile for Edinburgh West, using the 2011 census information. See www.constituencyexplorer.org.uk
13. See – http://www.edinburghnews.scotsman.com/news/42m-project-for-700-new-homes-to-revive-muirhouse-1-3317570
14. There was an older Balfour Street in Leith, just off Leith Walk, which might explain the absence of a Balfour street name in Drumbrae.
15. There's even a Stevenson Way that repeats the route of Kidnapped from Mull to Edinburgh see http://www.stevensonway.org.uk
16. http://www.bbc.co.uk/news/uk-scotland-scotland-politics-29569585
17. If you want a flavour then consult David Torrance's referendum diary, *100 Days of Hope And Fear*, p. 143 for the Bufton Tufton party.
18. See http://www.womenforindependence.org
19. See http://nationalyesregistry.scot
20. See the two measures of independence in Christopher Carmen, Robert Johns and James Mitchell (2014), *More Scottish than British: The 2011 Scottish Parliament Election*, London: Palgrave, p.99.

21. Scottish Government (2016), *Scotland's Place in Europe*, Edinburgh: Scottish Government.

22. Scottish National Party (2016), *Re-elect* Manifesto, Edinburgh: SNP, p.24.

23. This phrase refers to the type of political/economic problem that seems intractable and/or highly difficult to resolve.

24. These figures came from YouGov opinion polls on 9th November 2014 and 2nd February 2015. Before undecideds were excluded Yes was at 48 per cent to 45 per cent and 49 per cent to 44 per cent.

25. Ipsos-MORI poll for STV, 2nd September 2015.

26. http://www.tns-bmrb.co.uk/news/snp-lead-eases-but-support-for-independence-rises-a-year-after-referendum

27. http://tns-bmrb.co.uk/news/snp-holds-poll-lead-in-spite-of-mixed-views-on-record-in-government

28. See the Survation poll of 14th July 2015, reported on here: http://blog.whatscotlandthinks.org/2015/07/survation-on-the-opportunities-and-challenges-of-2016/

29. See table in http://whatscotlandthinks.org/questions/how-would-you-vote-in-the-in-the-scottish-independence-referendum-if-held-now-a#table

30. See table of data at http://whatscotlandthinks.org/questions/if-a-majority-of-people-in-the-uk-voted-for-the-uk-to-leave-the-eu-how-would-yo#table

31. This last poll was by YouGov at http://whatscotlandthinks.org/questions/how-would-you-vote-in-the-in-a-scottish-independence-referendum-if-held-now-ask#table

32. BMG poll for *The Herald,* 2nd January 2017, p.1.

33. Poll by Ipsos- MORI for STV, 4th March 2017.

34. See http://whatscotlandthinks.org/questions/how-would-you-vote-in-the-in-a-scottish-independence-referendum-if-held-now-ask#table

35. See Jamie Maxwell, 'The East Renfrewshire Problem', http://bellacaledonia.org.uk/2016/05/12/the-east-renfrewshire-problem/

36. This phrase refers to the type of political/economic problem that seems intractable and/or highly difficult to resolve.

37. https://www.opendemocracy.net/uk/peter-geoghegan-adam-ramsay/you-aren-t-allowed-to-know-who-paid-for-key-leave-campaign-adverts

38. See the blog by Women for Independence here, which certainly chimed with a lot of my experience on the doorsteps - http://www.womenforindependence.org/how_do_we_persuade_women_to_support_independence?platform=hootsuite

Bibliography

Adamson, Kevin and Peter Lynch (2014) (Eds), *Political Parties and the Scottish Independence Referendum 2014*, Cardiff: Welsh Academic Press.

Bremner, Stewart (2015), *The Early Days of a Better Nation*, Edinburgh: Imagined Images Editions.

Carman, Christopher, Robert Johns and James Mitchell (2014), *More Scottish than British? The 2011 Scottish Parliament Election*, London: Palgrave.

Cochrane, Alan (2014), *Alex Salmond: My Part in his Downfall*, London: Biteback.

Common Weal (2017), *The White Paper Project: Version 1.0*, Glasgow: Common Weal.

Curtice, John and Rachel Ormston (2012), *Scottish Independence: The state of the Union: public opinion and the Scottish question*, British Social Attitudes, 29.

Dalzell, Craig (2017), *The Demographics of Independence*, Glasgow: Common Weal.

Ford, Robert and Matthew Goodwin (2014), *Revolt on the Right: Explaining Support for the Radical Right in Britain*, London: Routledge.

Geoghegan, Peter (2015), *The People's Referendum: Why Scotland Will Never Be the Same Again*, Edinburgh: Luath Press.

Higgins, Kate (2014), *Generation Scot Y*, Edinburgh: Luath Press.

McAlpine, Robin (2016), *Determination*, Glasgow: Common Weal.

Maxwell, Stephen (2012), *Arguing for Independence: Evidence, Risk and the Wicked Issues*, Luath Press: Edinburgh.

Robertson, James (2014), *365 Stories*, London: Hamish Hamilton.

Salmond, Alex (2014), *The Dream Shall Never Die*, London: William Collins

Stevenson, Robert Louis (2012), *Kidnapped*, London: Vintage Books.

Sullivan, William (2014), *The Missing Scotland: Why Over a million Scots choose not to vote and what it means for our democracy*, Edinburgh: Luath Press.

Torrance, David (2014), *100 Days of Hope And Fear*, Edinburgh: Luath Press.

Welsh, Irvine (2001), *Trainspotting*, London: Vintage Books.